DINING IN THE DARK

DINING IN THE DARK

DINING IN THE DARK

A Famed Restaurant Critic's Struggle with and Triumph over Depression

BRYAN MILLER

Skyhorse Publishing

Skyhorse Publishing books may be purchased in bulk at special discounts for sales promotion, corporate gifts, fund-raising, or educational purposes. Special editions can also be created to specifications. For details, contact the Special Sales Department, Skyhorse Publishing, 307 West 36th Street, 11th Floor, New York, NY 10018 or info@skyhorsepublishing.com.

Skyhorse® and Skyhorse Publishing® are registered trademarks of Skyhorse Publishing, Inc.®, a Delaware corporation.

Visit our website at www.skyhorsepublishing.com.

10 9 8 7 6 5 4 3 2 1

Library of Congress Cataloging-in-Publication Data is available on file.

Cover design by Kai Texel

Print ISBN: 978-1-5107-6039-4
Ebook ISBN: 978-1-5107-6040-0

Printed in the United States of America

"Words are for what other people have been through, and nobody who has been through this particular experience has ever been able to convey it to anyone who hasn't, perhaps for the simple reason that it has no features to speak of. It is Nothing the Nth power; Nothing heightened to the screaming point."

—*Wilfrid Sheed*

TABLE OF CONTENTS

DINING IN THE DARK

DINING IN THE DARK

CHAPTER 1
The Beard Award

FOR THOSE GRAPPLING WITH DEPRESSIVE illness, life is largely about showing up. Social interactions can be exquisitely painful, and much of one's time is taken up contriving ways to avoid them. For more than a dozen years at the *New York Times*, my life was consumed by high-profile work and endless socializing. I reviewed restaurants five to six nights a week in the company of one or two couples; had lunch two to three days a week; reported food stories; wrote a weekly recipe column, a weekly kitchen equipment column, and magazine features; this was augmented by public speaking, a daily radio spot, and a weekly TV appearance. I am surprised they didn't draft me as an auxiliary truck driver. I held what was widely considered the best job in food journalism—indeed, the best job in the country, period. In the span of nine years as the *Times*' restaurant critic I dined out more than 5,100 times, not counting the company cafeteria and food trucks. Greater New York City was my peach—but it had a dark, moldy underside.

In 1982, I was felled by what might be called a double helping of mental illness. Typically, one is plagued either by a biochemical depression, caused by inexplicable changes in brain chemistry, or an emotional disturbance arising from personal loss, separation, anxiety, or other factors. We know a tremendous amount about the physical brain—how it communicates with various parts of the body, where information is stored, and how it responds to stimuli and medications.

But when it comes to the etiology of depression, the *why* it is torment-ing nearly one in five American adults as I write this sentence, there is so much to learn.

Remarkably, despite my dread of socializing, I never failed to show up for a restaurant review. At times I would stand at the front door, breathing heavily like a prizefighter before the bell, heart throbbing, brain on fire. I repeated to myself that I could do it, had done so hun-dreds of times, and that it would pass quickly. It could take a while, but I always went in.

Outside of professional eating, however, there were numerous vanish-ing acts, from the minor (private dinner parties, sports events, work func-tions) to the major (media interviews, business travel, social engagements). To this day I suspect there are some incensed Canadians in Ottawa who, in 1993, invited me to be the keynote speaker at a big gourmet gala, four hundred guests. It sounded like fun five months in advance—as do many such invitations—until the date approaches. Crushingly depressed, I made it as far as the United Airlines boarding gate.

Taking a seat near the ticketing desk, I weighed the consequences of going to Ottawa versus not going to Ottawa. If I were to go, and suffer through the event, delivering a halting, semi-coherent speech, at least I would find two thousand dollars in my pocket. Going straight home, on the other hand, would be capitulating to the disease. As the last stragglers trundled through the gate, the attendant, a middle-aged lady with tight hair and a pinched smile, turned to me. Was I on this flight?

"No, no, I made a mistake. It's the next one."

Three years into the illness, and between wives, I had drifted far from the shores of optimism regarding an imminent cure. The medi-cations—anywhere from seventy to 114 pills a week—could be like an overmatched prizefighter, effective in the early rounds but ultimately weak-kneed and feckless. At times they left me a trembling, withered old man. Climbing the stairs to my third floor apartment could be a five minute trek. Psychotherapy was bearing some fruit, though as yet barely enough to make a small cobbler. Grimly, I came to expect the worst, and it was worse than I expected.

In 1991, the James Beard Foundation anointed me with one of its two highest honors, the James Beard Foundation's *Who's Who of Food & Beverage in America*, awarded to a "most accomplished food and beverage professional in the country." I had been at the *Times* for just over six years, five as the restaurant critic. It seemed a little early to get a career tribute like that, sort of like being voted into the National Baseball Hall of Fame when your rookie contract runs out. The honor came with a large bronze trophy the weight of a young St. Bernard, in the form of a French waiter.

The Beard Foundation, a non-profit culinary organization that likens itself to the motion picture academy, bestows annual awards to chefs, restaurateurs, wine professionals, journalists, and other industry types. It started in the mid-1980s with a couple of dozen honors and was put on in a hotel. Today it is nearly out of control, a Woodstock of self-congratulations. Fueled by corporate sponsorships and media hype, it runs on for days and attracts foodies from as far as Hawaii. In 2017, medals were bestowed upon many dozens of chefs, restaurants, and media.

The Beard Foundation is not alone. Over the past thirty years the food and wine industry has become a Santa's sack of tributes and prizes: the S. Pellegrino "Almost Famous" Chef award, the Food Service Consultants award, the International Food & Beverage Forum award, the Master of Aesthetics of Hospitality Award, and National Restaurant Association's Kitchen Innovation Award Lamb Jam (I do not know what it is either). One gets the impression that today, if you are in a position of some authority in the food business, and hang in there long enough without conspicuously embarrassing yourself, it is hard not to win a prize. I stopped attending the Beard awards in the early 1990s. Sitting that long, my ass went numb.

Two days before the event I was browsing in a guitar shop near Times Square. A familiar bell chimed in my brain. First there was a tingling on the surface of the scalp, like a mild electrical current; then confusion, followed by great anxiety. Before long, a cognitive thunderstorm rolled in, knocking down power lines and making a mess of things. My racing thoughts were random and unfocused and frightening ... the wonderful assortment of guitars hanging on the walls could have been cured hams. I was certain I had forgotten how to play, so what was I doing there? I wanted to go home and sleep until it passed, but that was wishful thinking. In its wake arrived a thick, gauzy fog—a dull, stultifying nothingness that Emily Dickenson described as a so-called "funeral in the brain."

At the time I was taking an ornery medication called Nardil. It is a Monoamine Oxidase Inhibitor (MAO), among the first antidepressants, developed in the 1950s. MAOs elevate levels of the neurotransmitters norepinephrine, serotonin, and dopamine, all related to mood. Surprisingly, it is often the drug of choice when modern medications prove ineffective. MAOs have fallen out of favor because of potentially dangerous interactions with certain foods, drinks, and other medications—perfect for a food writer. It is risky when combined with the chemical tyramine, an amino acid that helps regulate blood pressure and is found in red wine, aged cheeses, some smoked meats and fish, and more. They say it is in caviar, but I was not about to accept that without a fight. One day at home I consumed a teaspoon of Beluga (the highest grade) hoping I would not have to dial 911. Fortunately, I was fine, and continued to experiment with more generous (and expensive) servings to no ill effect.

Aged cheese is another matter; on one occasion, after an accidental ingestion of feta cheese in a salad, my blood pressure skyrocketed, sending me into near stroke territory. I was trundled out of the *Times* newsroom on a gurney and hospitalized overnight. I have always wondered which of my colleagues observed this loud and unscripted performance, and why no one ever mentioned it.

It so happened that, on the day I began taking Nardil, I arrived at the office and bumped into Frank Prial, our wine critic. A ruddy Irishman with a generous girth and a pocketful of witticisms, he was an immensely popular columnist because of his down-to-earth, witty writing style and approachable erudition.

"Bryan, come on up to the test kitchen and help out," he beckoned. "I'm tasting some Beaujolais."

All Beaujolais is red.

I determined it was some sort of leap of faith I needed to go through and joined him. Besides, professional wine tasters do not drink the wine; rather, they swirl it around in the mouth, swallow a little, and spit it out. So I swirled, sniffed, tasted and expectorated for half an hour. It turned out that red wine, like caviar, was not a problem for me. Nor were white or rosé. What a relief.

Prial was also a talented reporter, having held at least a dozen positions at the paper over the years, including Paris correspondent. He wanted off the vinous beat, chiefly so he could return to Paris. If that were to happen, the paper would need a new wine writer. The brass decided I was a suitable palette and requested I accompany Frank on his bibulous rounds, which could involve assessing several dozen wines a day. How great was that? Drinking for a living. The paper even enrolled me in wine school.

It did not take long to discover that my antidepressant Nardil was a real party pooper. At higher doses, it drains the libido to the level of an octogenarian, which is problematic for a married thirty-nine-year old male. Thirty milligrams, an average dose, leaves the engine difficult to turn over; at 45mg it sputters and belches smoke; at 60mg it repeatedly stalls out; 75mg, well, you can imagine. In the early days, I was prescribed 90mg.

My Beard Award appearance was set for 9:00 p.m., when I was expected to take to the rostrum and scatter some pearls of gastronomic wisdom. I would have rather been buried alive. Shortly after 7:00 p.m., I dressed in a charcoal suit and a loud yellow tie that had been presented to me by Pierre Troisgros, a three-star French chef. Adorning the tie were images of Pierre's restaurant and his team of cooks—pretty wild, but that was the only night I could wear it without looking tacky.

The event was held at the Times Square Marriott Marquis hotel, which has a grand ballroom that could hold a medium-sized junior college. I thought about the dozens of strange foodies I would encounter; the bubbly networking; the vows to get together for dinner, which of course we would not. Then there were those pearls of wisdom. I had scratched out a few talking points on a paper menu from a Japanese noodle parlor, but that hardly comprised pearls of anything. The night would be beyond distressing, presuming I could pull it off at all. Then again, there was the unthinkable: I could bail.

"No, you can't do that," I admonished myself. The entire culinary world will be there: the food press, colleagues from the *Times*, restaurant owners, chefs, and industry leaders. *If you bail, it will be a calamity for the Beard Foundation, and for you.*

Turning west on 52nd Street, amid the forest of glass towers lining the Avenue of the Americas, I approached a popular steakhouse called Ben Benson's. I had never reviewed the place, although it was well-regarded and only three blocks from my apartment, so I don't know why I hadn't. The tanned and tweedy namesake owner enjoyed a wide and loyal following. I had stopped by two years prior while researching the best crab cakes in New York. Ben Benson's was the runaway winner—enormous, with sweet fresh crab, no filler, encased in a latticework of golden brittle potatoes. (Lamentably, the restaurant closed in 2012, and Mr. Benson died in 2020.)

Near the entrance was a small, clubby bar that saw a flash flood of financial executives when the corporate whistle sounded at 5:00 p.m. I felt very weak, from torpor or tension, and decided to have a quick drink. By 6:30 p.m. the crowd was thinning out as tipplers hustled to catch trains to Larchmont or Tarrytown or Scarsdale. I commandeered a stool, reckoning that if I got myself sufficiently embalmed the evening might pass with less angst. I glanced at the clock: 7:10 p.m. The event had commenced at the Marriott.

I was not exactly in the mood for barroom badinage, but the loud tie invited several queries regarding my plans for the evening. "You're looking' sharp, sir," remarked a burly fellow in his forties, wearing a khaki suit and a blonde brush cut. He had probably played defensive end in college.

"Nice tie," he added. "Where are you off to?"

"Nowhere," I mumbled.

"So you are all dressed up with no place to go?"

"I guess so. I'm supposed to be somewhere, but it's a long story."

"Women. Say no more."

Two older fellows at the end of the bar nodded in approbation. The man introduced himself as Gregory. My heart was racing. I needed a drink, and ordered a rye old fashioned, my favorite cocktail. An interesting looking man soon arrived; he was tall, trim, in his sixties, with longish salt-and-pepper hair and a slow, warm smile. Clearly European. His name was Roger—actually, Rogier, from Belgium. He was nattily attired in a dark blue suit, Turnbull and Asser checked shirt, and blue tie. Time had skied down Rogier's face, etching verti-cal creases that, in most men, would telegraph age but only added to his dignified mien. He could have been an art curator, a diplomat, an international banker. One thing was for sure: whatever Rogier was, he was well acquainted with that bar and the other patrons.

He told me he was in the shipping business—fats and oils, whatever that meant.

"Off to some fun party tonight?" he asked, inspecting my tie.

"No."

"Me either. I'm supposed to be at a gala at the Norwegian Consu-late—it's Norwegian Independence Day, did you know that?"

"No," I confessed. "Independence from whom?"

"The Danes. After four centuries."

"Are you going to the gala?"

"Hell no … those crazy sons-a-bitches drink like it's judgment day; too much for me. I used to drink like it was judgment day. For thirty years, like everybody in shipping. Not anymore—surprised I'm alive."

Rogier explained how, until the late 1970s, virtually all business in commercial shipping was conducted in bars and restaurants. "That's the way it had always been, and that's how I came up in the business," he said, ordering a Scotch. He recounted how representatives of various interests—brokers, agents, ship stewards—met in a restaurant around noon, sometimes in groups, or one on one. There they would convene, liberally irrigated by a barman who knew the routine so well he could perform it in the dark. The drinking and horse trading went on until about 4:00 p.m.

And you still had a productive day?

"We'd go back to the office, make a few phone calls, then return to the bar for more work and dinner."

Sedated by two muscular old fashioneds, my brain still felt sheathed in gauze. Psychiatrists strongly admonish patients taking antidepressants to steer clear of alcohol. For the vast majority of depressed people who attempt to drink themselves out of their misery, booze is an exit door painted on the wall. Alcohol is a central nervous system depressant, and overdoing it can make one feel worse. In one respect I am fortunate, for I have a bell in my head that rings when I have reached my limit. Beyond that, I can be terribly sick for days. So I never cross the line. (Although that night came close.)

Nearly a third of people suffering from major depression have a drinking problem to some degree. Women are more than twice as likely to start drinking excessively if they have a history of depression. Teens that have had one bout of major depression are twice as likely to start drinking as those who have not. And, if they are on medication, there could be serious side effects.

Again, I entertained the idea of blowing off the award ceremony.

No, you can't do that. The entire culinary world will be there: the food press, colleagues from the Times, *restaurant owners, chefs, industry leaders. If you bail it will be a calamity for the Beard Foundation, and for you.*

I bailed.

My third cocktail was taxiing down the runway, donated by Rogier.

The Beard Awards were no longer heavy on my mind, as long as I did not look at the clock.

I looked at the clock.

8:30 p.m.

If I changed my mind, there was still time to shuffle down to the Marriot and make an ass of myself. I turned my attention to the new old fashioned. Then arrived a hefty fellow named Martin, an affable Irishman from Westchester who was in the commercial real estate business. He was one of the regulars, with an earnest smile and firm salesman's handshake. He exhibited little urgency to decamp to his hushed suburban hideaway. Rogier, too, appeared to be settled in for the later innings, while deliberating another martini.

Gregory had recently moved with his wife and ten-year-old son from Manhattan to northern Westchester. He explained that it was not his initiative, but he had been out-voted.

"Bought a house," he huffed. "It's true—they *are* money pits. And so much work." Then there are the taxes, he added. And having to drive everywhere.

On the other hand, he allowed, there were benefits to the placid country life.

"You know, I think I'll get to like it," he said. He said it three times.

We went on talking about everything, mostly sports and restaurants. And dogs.

"I had a red setter when I lived in Fairfield," recalled Rogier. He explained that he was the "goddamn stupidest" animal he'd ever seen. He liked to sleep under the coffee table, and if the kids came in making loud noises, he would jump up, whacking his head, every time. It was comforting to spend time with some blokes who knew little about neither my world nor my illness and just wanted to shoot the breeze. I was invisible. No one could intrude upon my scary world.

After the third old fashioned, the Beard Awards had faded into the mist. I was not drunk, but I was not sober. The three of us called it a night and promised to see each other soon.

The following morning I was in possession of what the French call a "guele de bois" (wooden mouth). A sequoia. And that was the least of my penance. I suffered from a nuclear headache and a royally vindictive stomach. Coffee offered little relief. The refrigerator was bare, save for a package of Kodak film and a roll of rock hard goat cheese.

At 9:00 a.m. I headed down to the office—something I tried to avoid when depressed, but today there was an important story meeting. As I approached the Marriott Marquis, images of the awards ceremony played out in my mind. In my fantasy, all the preliminary medals had been passed out. The largely inebriated audience awaited the grand event.

"And now," the president of the James Beard Foundation beamed, "the award for *Who's Who of Food & Beverage in America* is Bryan Miller of the *New York Times.* "

Hearty applause.

The recipient should be on his way to the stage.

More hearty applause.

Where is the recipient?

Lackluster applause.

Heads begin turning toward the rear of the ballroom.

No applause. Murmurings. The foundation president sheepishly waits at the podium, an unclaimed bronze statue gleaming under the spotlights.

Turning onto West 43rd Street, I entered the *Times* building and made a detour to my desk in order to avoid eye contact with the food staff. Would they confront me as a chastising group, or individually? And even if they left me to myself, would I be fielding calls from food journalists around the country?

To my astonishment, no one brought up the Beard Award.

Following the editorial meeting, at which I contributed two good story proposals, I scooted out of the building, vowing to stay clear of the office for a while. Being a senior *Times* critic—I think there were around seven on the paper—I was a privileged character, free to come and go as I pleased as long as I fed the lion twice a week.

The question was, what do I do about my shameful dereliction? What a slap in the face to the foundation. They must want to hog-tie me to a pickup truck and drag me around Times Square. I considered going down to the foundation's headquarters to apologize, but what would I say? I am a manic depressive and you caught me on a bad day? Better perhaps to craft a letter of groveling apology. Still, what was the reason? Depressed people lie about their condition all the time, but for once in my life my lie repository was coming up dry. Looking back, I should have done something. I subsequently learned that Florence Fabricant, a *Times* food reporter, was nice enough to (awkwardly) accept the award on my behalf. We have never discussed it.

Two months later I was enjoying a beer on the porch of my farmhouse in Rhinebeck, NY, about ninety miles north of Manhattan along the Hudson River, savoring a glorious stretch of well-being. It was a resplendent autumn afternoon. A UPS truck pulled up the driveway and the courier placed at my feet a large, heavy, cardboard box. I lugged it inside and sawed through the top with a bread knife, plunging my hands into bubble wrap. I lifted its content and placed it on the kitchen table.

It was the trophy.

CHAPTER 2
The Black Bear

THE MORNING I TUMBLED INTO the jaws of mental illness, in November 1983, was ordinary in every way. As was my routine, I arose early to peruse the newspapers before commencing the work day. I wedged into my little office, which was the size of a rich man's shoe closet, and settled onto a swivel chair that lacked space to swivel. Upon scanning the front page of the *New York Times* it was evident that something was awry. I found myself reading the same paragraphs over and over. Everything was slow and opaque, like awakening after anesthesia.

It could not be a hangover. Anne, my girlfriend, and I had shared a bottle of wine the previous evening, which was not uncommon in our household. Attributing my condition to fatigue—I had been working long days writing freelance articles for the *New York Times* and other publications—I returned to bed. An hour later, with Anne rattling around in the kitchen, I padded into the office. It was worse. I was trapped in a gauzy mental haze. It was as if a mischievous visitor had sneaked in and lowered the light dimmer in my brain.

Reading was possible but slow and soon forgotten; writing was out of the question. My heart began pounding. For the remainder of the day the light dimmer remained at low. Unable to work, I passed the time with mindless tasks—organizing files, polishing copper pans, running errands—with the expectation of doubling down the following day.

On Friday morning I remained in bed until after eight, a rarity, while Anne started her day. Recumbent on the futon—we could not afford a proper bed at the time—I had the premonitory feeling that the day would not embrace me with a smile. Happily, for the first five minutes my mind was as clear as a winter's dawn, and I tried to discount the previous day's drama. Perhaps it had been an allergic reaction to the wine, or something I ate. I rose with a bounce in my step and a heightened appreciation for the normal.

Then came the ominous tapping on the back of the neck, followed by another swift descent into confusion and anxiety. It was like nothing I had ever experienced. I could not see it; I could not touch it; I could not really describe it; I had no idea how to fix it. It was like taking your car to the mechanic because "something is not working right." For the rest of the morning I remained in the office, feet on the desk, gazing over ice-glazed Long Island Sound.

A year before, Anne and I had moved into our snug two-bedroom cottage in Westport, Connecticut, overlooking an inlet of Long Island Sound. In the early 1980s, it was a quaint, neighborly, waterside village, affluent, but nothing like today, where Maseratis on Main Street barely merited a glance up from one's macchiato. Most businesses were folksy and locally owned. The cynosure of downtown's skyline was the beloved Pink Bookstore, set in a crazy, angular, low-ceilinged, colonial home.

The cottage's owners, George and Betty Malisk, who shared the same property, stipulated that the house was for married couples only. That proved little inconvenience, as we promptly self-nuptualized and moved in. The arrangement worked out fine, as they became quite fond of us, and we of them. Naturally, we kept conversations of the connubial nature under the table. That is, until we decided to tie the knot legally, and with a grand spring party. On our front lawn.

"You tell them," I implored Anne.

"No, you tell them."

"You tell them."

"Why?"

"Because you're a woman. They won't holler at you as much!"

Anne was gone for a good ten minutes, which could have meant anything. She finally returned, betraying no verdict.

"Well, well?" I asked, expecting the worst.

"They cried."

The cottage was magical, even in winter, when the cove froze over and tall, wispy reeds swayed in the wind like supple ballerinas. On clear days we could see the north shore of Long Island. Without doubt, those were the happiest days of my life. I was unaware that a monstrous tidal surge would soon drag me out to sea.

In love, and with similar interests and creative aspirations, Anne and I created a gastronomic cottage industry on secluded Hideaway Lane. Together we penned food columns for the *Hartford Courant*'s brassy new Sunday magazine, *Northeast*, with Anne cooking and calling out measurements, and me taking notes, writing the text, and overeating. At times our home resembled a boarding house, with local friends, some starving artist types, dropping by to avail themselves of whatever was simmering in our journalistic stockpot. We also reviewed restaurants for the magazine and reported food stories for various publications. Anne, a former Berlitz teacher, patiently schooled me in her native tongue. In a short six months I could confidently order a croissant in a French bakery, and ask a waiter for the wine list, which I did not understand.

Our compensation from *Northeast* was $450 a week and we earned nearly that writing for the *Times* and other publications. One day an editor from the publishing house Clarkson Potter called to ask Anne if she would like to help a local caterer put together a cookbook. Her name was Martha Stewart. Martha resided a couple of miles from us in her much photographed farmhouse on Turkey Hill Road, bounded by flawlessly manicured vegetable gardens and endless splays of flowers. She was affable, tireless, and easy to work with. The money was good, too.

As food journalists go, we were on a roll. Notwithstanding that we had been food scribes for only a short time, we sensed that big things were on the horizon. Actually, we were sure of it. Yet, for my part, those big things could wait. We were young and inspired, living by the sea, blessed with caring friends, appreciated for our work, and pretty much free to set our own schedules. That was a time to treasure. As I remarked to Anne, so many people experience the "best days of our lives" in retrospect. We were living it and appreciating it every day.

The world of culinary journalism that we entered was, by today's standards, straightforward and educational. Everything was new: truffles, morels, sea urchins, free-range chicken, foie gras, Japanese beef, confit, hand-harvested scallops, game, shiitake mushrooms, exotic French cheeses. California wines, long considered something that came in a jug, were making remarkable strides. Our job was to demystify new ingredients and techniques and come up with recipes for home cooks. It was great fun. Until the ceiling fell in.

Depression was not really on my radar, mostly because I knew little about it other than that it was either biochemical in nature, or situational—the death of a loved one, illness, a breakup. About a week into my malady, panic moved in. Every miserable day was the same, like prison without a defense attorney to boost your spirits. Having no one to talk with—I did not want to alarm Anne at that point—I drove down to the Greenwich library, which was the best in the area—and the only one in Fairfield County with computers, rudimentary as they were at the time—and pulled out some books on mental illness. Sitting on the floor, I skimmed them looking for answers. Most expounded more or less the same thing and posed questions that remain unresolved today: why has modern science, which can identify a miniscule spot in the brain that sparks epilepsy or Parkinson's disease not yet located that pesky depression gene? And why does the illness come and go as it pleases, without warning, not even the courtesy of a phone call?

Then my ailment took a curious turn. I would feel normal for four days, crash for the same time, and then return to normal. The fleeting escape from the haze was welcome and promising. Was the depression breaking up, like an ice flow? I clung to this belief like an infant to a comfy blanket, only to find that it had merely run out to the store and would soon return.

One of the library's textbooks devoted a chapter to manic depression, which was known to most people in its exaggerated almost caricature form. In it, one falls into the abyss for days or longer and then blasts off to a neuron-charged nirvana. The highs can occasion hyperactive comportment, rash decision making, and at times reckless financial behavior, like trying to purchase Grant's Tomb on a Visa card. It came out that my disorder resembled what is called Bipolar 2, or unipolar depression. As such, I rode the elevator to the sub-basement, passed some time in the dark and cold, then returned to the ground floor. The levels above—where the party was in full swing—never saw me. Individuals who ascend to manic depression's giddy heights sometimes describe it as a state of super clarity, even elation—and look forward to its return. I felt cheated.

In subsequent weeks, I strove to display an upbeat disposition in front of Anne, which was like humming Beatles' tunes during an amputation. After all, I still held hope that it could flare out, so why alarm her? It was not as if Anne were unacquainted with tragedy. As a teenager she lost her mother to suicide; while on a Riviera vacation she leaped from a hotel window—in front of Anne. Anne lived for a time with her pious, soft-spoken father at the family estate, called Soustres, in the Languedoc region of France, a fifteen bedroom structure in a speck of a village called Montady that is not far from the historic city of Bezier. The core of the house is believed to have been built around the thirteenth century. (The fireplace, about the size of a Manhattan studio apartment, still functions, although it needs a chimney sweeping every century or so). Soustres is now partitioned into three residences, one for each branch of the family. Anne's full name is Anne de Ravel d'Esclapon, which to a Frenchman is impressive indeed, as it goes far back in French history. There is even a little town in Provence called

Esclapon, although I have never been there. In the 1980s, the family at Soustres enjoyed more space than income, and the homespun interior was far from Downton Abbey.

I met Anne in Washington, DC, when she was a supervisor at Berlitz. I had driven down from Easton, Connecticut, where I was an editor at *Connecticut Magazine*, to spend the Fourth of July weekend with a longtime friend, Nancy, a tall, lovely half-French woman whom I had known for more than ten years. We had never been intimate, although it remained within the sphere of possibility.

A natural organizer, Nancy had arranged a picnic for a group of friends on the greensward below the United States Capitol to watch the fireworks. While sipping white wine with expensive cheeses, I was informed that a "young French girl who did not have many friends in town" would be joining us. Within five minutes of her arrival she had found a doting friend: me. I don't know what possessed me, but I rudely ignored Nancy and the others and focused *all* attention on Anne.

Anne is as French looking as it gets—pick your cliché—with fair skin, lively eyes, a cute, angular nose, and a decorative mole above the upper lip. I have always been curious about why some foreigners learn English and easily shed their native accents, while others do not. Anne is in the latter group. I have joked that after more than thirty years in the States she still spoke as if she were passing through United States Customs for the first time. For the rest of the day I followed her around like a dog. When it was time to leave, I discarded Nancy like a spent sparkler and took flight with Anne. It is one of the most shameful things I have ever done, and presaged my callous behavior with women—illness driven but inexcusable nonetheless—for years to come. Four decades later I think of it often.

Anne had moved to Washington three years prior to put some distance between her and the appalling family tragedy. Like many French women, she was refined and self-effacing, exceedingly feminine in both dress and demeanor. She would no sooner walk to work in sneakers carrying a backpack than stride down Madison Avenue on stilts. Several years later, when we lived in midtown Manhattan, on 55th Street off Fifth Avenue, if she had to run out to the corner deli, she would dress as if it were date night, including lipstick. I loved it.

CHAPTER 3
Spain

SHORTLY BEFORE MEETING ANNE I was in preparation for an educational sabbatical in Europe, part of my life philosophy of taking a personal year every five to six years. I had little money but much youth, and wanted to see some of the globe before work, family, and other life anchors slowed me down. A little research yielded an exhilarating itinerary: hop a tramp steamer to Casa Blanca and then make my way across Morocco to the Straits of Gibraltar. From there I would head up to Algeciras, Spain, and on to the magnificent city of Renaissance Salamanca, where I would enroll in language school.

I could not afford, nor did I care to, make the crossing on a gluttonous passenger liner. The wheezing, rust-dappled *Tuhobic*, flying a Yugoslav flag, held the raw Conradian allure I was looking for. Tramp steamers were the Uber services of the high seas, summoned to different ports to fetch cargo, often on short notice, so you were never sure where you would wind up nor for how long. Passage to Casa Blanca was normally ten days, for $350 apiece, regardless how long we would spend on the high seas. Our voyage was seventeen exhilarating days.

Although I hardly knew Anne at the time, and had planned the trip as my solo Lewis and Clark expedition, she kept after me, saying that she wanted to attend a family wedding in France (which she missed). I cannot help think about how her life would have been far better if she had not ascended the gangplank in Baltimore, and instead let me drift out of her world.

On the ship we shared a sizable stateroom, all varnished wood with stainless steel trim. There was a large porthole at water level, ideal for experimenting with sea sickness. Fortunately, the ocean was cooperative as we crossed the Atlantic except for one rock and roll evening when it was challenging to stand at the officers' bar—even when stabilized by numerous shots of jenever, a sinus-clearing, juniper flavored Dutch liquor.

The ship hauled anchor for Casa Blanca on September 25, a brilliant day under a cerulean sky. As we passed into the open ocean, Anne and I stood at the bow's railing, arm in arm, the salty breeze in our faces, like Kate Winslet and Leonardo DiCaprio in *Titanic*.

Our first port of call was the unexciting Norfolk Naval Station, on Chesapeake Bay, where we remained for two days to unload some cargo. From there the ship was summoned to Savannah, Georgia to fetch four giant cargo containers, miles of black cable, and a new Toyota. For four days we explored the enchanting southern city and its hefty cuisine. In mid-September, it was over a hundred degrees, the air as heavy as a sea chest. Our tourism was limited to half hour walks broken up by equal time in over-air conditioned bars. Still, it was thrilling to be there—and on a romantic Leninist vessel no less—and we would not have minded if the next port were Tierra del Fuego.

Docked nearby was a sleek, colossal Russian cruise ship. Our sailors challenged the Russian crew to a soccer match. It was insisted I participate, notwithstanding that a soccer ball had never touched my toes. We prevailed, owing to a superior defense and, no doubt, my moral encouragement. At a celebration party below deck that night—on a tramp steamer every night is a party—I had the opportunity to speak with some of the sailors, many of whom spoke halting English. Virtually all complained about Yugoslavia's Communist government and the struggling economy. For them sailing into American ports like Savannah was a dream. Two young sailors confided that they yearned to defect. One did, but I don't know where it occurred. Morocco I suppose.

On a hot, still morning, the *Tuhobic* wedged through a dense, dust-orange haze and into the port of Casablanca. I had never been to North Africa—actually, I had never traveled farther than Oklahoma—and it was absolutely galvanizing. A pair of friendly Moroccan customs agents extended their hospitality by confiscating my cameras and refusing to give them back. I made a scene, and disclosed that I was a journalist. That made it worse. For half an hour there was mumbling and passing around of my expensive equipment. I remarked to Anne they were probably discussing which items would make nice Ramadan gifts for their children. I continued to make such a ruckus that they returned the merchandise just to get rid of me.

Imagine tramping through a tunnel of swarming locusts, shirtless. That is how it felt to be a young American tourist in Casablanca at that time. We were endlessly accosted by aggressive trinket peddlers, rug vendors, food purveyors and the worst, menacing adolescents taunting and threatening us to follow them into the teeming, pick-pocket paradise of the open market. Many of them spoke French, a vestige of France's former colonization of the country. Anne swatted away our pursuers with a few choice French epithets, but they always returned. I wanted to leave for Spain right away.

Instead we drove two-and-a-half hours south to Marrakech, a handsome medieval city known for its dense, labyrinthine streets and markets. We remained for a spectacular Moroccan dinner. It started with couscous, a cornmeal-like grain paired with succulent lamb (it is sometimes made with chicken) and vegetables, perfumed with cinnamon, saffron, ginger, and coriander. I could eat it every day. Following was b'steeya, a phyllo-topped savory pie, sprinkled with cinnamon and sugar, typically made with shredded chicken, almonds, and herbs. As an accompaniment we nibbled on terrific fried almonds scented with orange flower water. Travel literature emphatically cautioned visitors to avoid drinking the tap water. In the middle of the night I arose, extremely parched, and with no bottled water. A little sip from the tap could not hurt me, no? By sunrise I suffered an atomic case of diarrhea that raged for two days. We decided to hop the first ferry to Algeciras, Spain. From there I boarded a train to Salamanca while Anne set off for France, where she would peruse photos of her cousin's nuptials.

To enter the Plaza Mayor of Salamanca, considered the finest in all of Spain, is like falling out of a cloud and landing in the Renaissance. History is layered upon history like playing cards, and one could spend weeks peeking into its ancient churches and courtyards. It is a spirited college town going back to the founding of the University of Salamanca, one of the oldest universities in the world, circa 1134. For several hundred years it was among the foremost fonts of scholarship in Europe, particularly in the disciplines of philosophy and mathematics. To be a "Salamanca man" was an intellectual insignia of unmatched distinction. I just wanted to master the subjunctive tense in Spanish. Today the city is a magnet for language studies and college semesters abroad. Anne arrived in two weeks and enrolled as well. We studied for six months, although I am not certain if we attended more classes or tapas bars.

While I was unaware of my future calling as a food writer, I wrote detailed notes on the local gastronomy. Salamanca is in the heart of Castilla (Castile), an undulating, grassy land of bull fighting, rustic food, and inexpensive wine. There is great local pride in its world-renowned cured ham (serrano). The cuisine is definitely for carnivores. If you order a salad in a restaurant, the flummoxed waiter will return, after much discussion with the chef, with a plate of iceberg lettuce supporting a lifeless trio of canned asparagus. Maybe some olives thrown in. The most popular regional dish is roasted suckling pig (locally known as *tostón*), ineffably succulent and tender, with a glistening golden crust. This was an expensive indulgence for a student who came to town with two thousand dollars in his jeans for six months. Roasted lamb grilled over grape vines was equally sublime. Tapas bars displayed a wide selection of inexpensive *pinchos* (small plates) and *raciones* (larger portions): steamed mussels, shrimp in garlic sauce, Spanish omelets (made with potatoes and eggs), grilled sardines, clams in Romesco sauce (made with pimientos, garlic, blanched almonds, fried bread, dried chilis, and more), and an expensive delicacy that we sampled on our first and last days in Salamanca: angulas, thin baby eels from the Sargasso Sea, in sizzling garlic-infused olive oil. For students and other "pobres" like me there was one go-to tapa that was as peculiar as it was economical: "sangre," or blood. Resembling firm Jell-O, it can be made with the blood of a pig, a bull, a chicken, or even a sheep and is often flavored with onions and spices. It is, as they say, an acquired taste.

When our allotted time was up (when we were broke), we had little desire to return to Ronald Reagan's America. We practically had to crawl around our room for loose coins in order to finance a flight home. Then luck—suerte in Spanish—came out of the blue. Two months prior, as a lark, I sent out resumes to several newspapers that might have a need for a Spanish speaking reporter, even though I was far from fluent. To my surprise, the *Miami Herald* responded, quite enthusiastically, and even offered to fly us back to the newspaper.

They had called my bluff. Nonetheless, it was not a difficult decision. Connecticut in mid-winter was a pewter colored deep freezer. Miami seemed like paradise—palm trees, blue-green ocean, convertibles, Latin music, Caribbean food. Being unaware that my seamless psychological life was coming to an end, I was game for anything. At the *Herald* office I was, thankfully, greeted in English. I satisfactorily completed several writing exams and was offered a position on the spot, but not as a swashbuckling foreign correspondent. They offered me the position of food section editor *and* restaurant critic. I had forgotten about *that* crazy exaggeration in my application letter. I asked the editor-in-chief if we could linger for a couple of days to get the pulse of the metropolis.

The following morning we set out to explore the downtown area. It was anything but paradise. Many stores were shuttered. There was much lively Spanish language graffiti, boarded up homes and stores, and few pedestrians. If you were in the market for a charred automobile without tires, the inventory was boundless. It was the early 1980s and, as we discovered on that first day, Miami was the epicenter of illicit drugs, primarily cocaine and heroin, coming into the United States from South America by air and sea. This is when the term cartel entered the lexicon. The blood-stained drug trade resulted in a torrent of murders and violent crimes in South Florida, leading to a terrified populace and the exodus of many businesses.

Ever optimistic, we motored to the city's celebrated "Calle Ocho" for an authentic Cuban lunch and taste of the city's "island flair." As it turned out, the shabby, desolate Calle Ocho had all the flair of an airport lounge, and there were only a handful of restaurants. We had a so-so lunch in a half empty place called Malaga. From there we cruised up to Coconut Grove, a wealthy enclave. This was encouraging. It appeared to be vivacious, clean and colorful, and devoid of visible firearms. Anne was silent on the drive back to the hotel, which took us past some scary looking pawn shops and seedy bars displaying posters of all-but-nude female employees. As we approached the parking lot, Anne began to sob. We returned to Connecticut.

CHAPTER 4
Food Writers

OUR FALLBACK PLAN WAS TO hone our culinary skills—actually, hone my skills, as Anne was already an accomplished cook—and try to make a go of it as fulltime food writers. We resolved to find work in a refined restaurant in order to get a worm's eye view of the apple, so to speak. Luckily, our dear friends, Charley Van Over and Priscilla Martel, owned one of the best establishments in Connecticut, called Restaurant du Village, in the hamlet of Chester.

We spent seven months there, Anne in the dining room, and me in the kitchen taking orders from the occasionally sober Irish chef, John, and his assistant. It was a tremendous learning experience, one that every aspiring restaurant critic should have, though few do. There was a lot of plucking "beards" from mussels, prepping vegetables, making stocks, preparing simple sauces, and boning meat and poultry. Being a sedentary writer by trade, the first month of standing six hours a day reminded me of Sister Joanna in third grade, whose favored mode of discipline was having a wayward student stand in the corner alone, facing the wall, for two weeks. Or so it seemed.

The experience hardly qualified me as a chef, but it was enlightening regarding the mechanics of a restaurant, both inside and out of the kitchen. I learned that the difference between a great home cook and a professional chef is that the former can create an excellent dinner for six while a chef can do so for sixty, and at staggered intervals. And seeing first-hand how restaurant dishes are created made me a more informed critic. When something goes wrong, even today, I have a good sense of why and how it can be rectified.

If I aspired to write about dining, I reasoned, it would be valuable to familiarize myself with dining room service. I volunteered to be a waiter for a week—not a great idea. It may have been a genetic defect, I don't know, but I was incapable of matching dishes with the individuals who had ordered them. Not even close. Luckily, it was a relaxed country restaurant in famously polite Connecticut, where customers were forgiving and generous with gratuities regardless of competency. It came to the point where, on my order pad, I assigned physical characteristics to each diner: duck (man red nose), shrimp (lady dark tan). And even that was not foolproof. I once served salad after dessert. It was good to return to the kitchen.

Toward the end of our apprenticeship I had an idea for a food article, inspired by living in Europe. It concerned ten foods that Americans routinely purchased in supermarkets that could be prepared better and more cheaply at home: salad dressing, croutons, barbecue sauce, pancake mix, garlic bread, and more. I pitched this to half a dozen newspapers. All declined except the *Christian Science Monitor*, which offered fifty dollars for the piece but first inquired about my religious affiliation (I imagine that they have ceased doing this). I found the question off-putting, but fifty dollars was fifty dollars.

With our apprenticeship winding down, Anne and I decided to move to Westport. As we were packing I received a call from one Alex Ward, who was the editor of the food section at the *New York Times*. Was it a practical joke? No, he wanted the ten foods story, and fast, because another article had fallen through. That unlikely development underscored a belief I have held for many years: No matter how smart, well-schooled, energetic, or conscious you may be, or think you are, much of your success in life has to do with accidents of luck. If we had moved out a day earlier, the call would have gone unanswered, and my career forever altered. Working with the restaurant chef we produced the article in a fifteen-hour day. The following week it was displayed on the front page of the *Times'* food section. My foot, as they say, was in the door.

I became a regular contributor of articles on every aspect of the food world: chef profiles, recipes, business, science, wine, food trends, and more. Ward and his staff were exceedingly nice and mentoring in the ways of the exacting *Times*. I was healthy and ambitious, and turned out more stories than many staffers. After freelancing at the paper for a year, I heard intimations that I might be offered a fulltime position. Ward informed me that, while at the time there was no food reporter opening, they could keep me busy in the wings writing a variety of stories for the Style section, an umbrella that comprised home design, fashion, society news, and general lifestyle topics. That was daunting. On the other hand, I had spent time as a reporter at the Associated Press, and was quick on my feet. Perhaps as baptism under fire, the paper assigned me to cover stories about which I could not be more ignorant, like home design, architecture, art, even society balls.

Then there was the morning I found myself sitting in the East Side apartment of the fashion designer Geoffrey Beene, whom I had heard of but needed to research in the paper's library. I was to interview him about the interior design of his spacious four-bedroom flat. Gracious, amiable, and soft spoken, he served me iced tea and politely inquired about my background, journalistic and personal. Conversation turned to his somewhat florid dwelling.

Can I give you a little tour?

"Interesting" was the first word that came to mind as we crossed into the sizable dining room sheathed in expensive wallpaper depicting the French countryside. In fact it was the *only* word that came to mind. As a reporter I had learned that when you interview someone without adequate preparation, or any functional knowledge of the subject, you should prod the interviewee into talking about him or herself to buy time and figure out what to do.

How long have you lived here? Where were you born? Do you come from a large family?

Surely he recognized that there was a drowning individual in front of him.

"Do you write frequently about design for the *Times?*" asked Mr. Beene.

"Oh yes, a lot. " I replied. "No, I don't. This is the first time."

"Why don't we take another tour and I'll narrate."

How embarrassing. I scribbled rapidly as he essentially wrote the article for me. Two weeks later the lushly detailed story appeared on the front page of the Home section. Mr. Beene sent me a graceful thank you note.

A few weeks later I was sent to cover a charity ball at the Metropolitan Museum of Art. My mandate was to mingle with the city's social elite, write about the setting, describe some celebrities, and gather a couple of bon mots from prominent guests. This presented challenges on two fronts. I did not recognize a single rich person. As for the ladies' attire, a friend and *Times* fashion photographer, Bill Cunningham, knew everyone and everything and what they were wearing. In fact, *he* was one of the biggest celebrities at the affair. I clicked on my tape recorder and followed him around like a golf caddie.

Shortly thereafter my on-and-off depression began to cycle. Overnight it turned my work life upside down. When feeling well, I learned to stock the freezer with as many stories and columns as I could by working ten to twelve hours a day. When the crash came—and it always came—this would provide a week or so of nourishment.

In early December, I received a call from the *Times* informing me that I would soon be meeting with Arthur Gelb, the paper's formidable assistant managing editor who was in charge of "soft news," which comprised the entire culture report, including food. I should have been ecstatic. However all I could think of was entering his office, stupefied, inarticulate, and near mute, blowing the deal. Days before, calculation revealed that I should be feeling normal from the following Wednesday through Sunday—it was that precise. However the call did not come for six weeks. All I could do was pray.

CHAPTER 5
Abe and Arthur

"ARTHUR GELB WILL SEE YOU now," the secretary beckoned with the warmth of a district attorney.

That was the most important cross-examination on the path to employment at the *Times*. If I made the grade with Gelb, all that remained would be a pro forma get-together with the executive editor, Abe Rosenthal. But I had been warned that Gelb could be a handful. Like a dropped garden hose, the storied *Times* editor could take off in any direction.

My health was holding up—I was about three-fourths through my normal cycle. My hiring was anything but certain. It was the 1980s, and the American newspaper industry was in its final laps of puissance and profitability before being disemboweled by the internet. The *Times* was a wealthy corporation, and it could hire anyone from anywhere.

I was directed to a spacious, photo-lined office overlooking the Theater District on West 44th Street. Gelb had once served as one of the paper's drama critics, and the walls were festooned with memorabilia and photos of show-biz luminaries past and present. Mostly past. I had seen the redoubtable Gelb on several occasions when I was visiting the newsroom, and was once introduced to him. Over the years he came to be a treasured friend, a mentor, colleague, father confessor, morale booster, marriage counselor, disciplinarian, and creative muse.

In short, I owe pretty much everything I have achieved as a journalist, and more, to him.

In subsequent years, after I had confided in him about my illness, I could speak freely. When emotions gummed up the gears at work, he was understanding but at the same time adamant about my soldiering through it, at whatever pace I could muster. He once disclosed that depression had visited his family, too, in current and past generations.

Gelb pretty much ran the newsroom along with Rosenthal. In fact, everyone referred to the *Times* as the "Abe and Arthur show." At the time Gelb's purview included the arts, style, food, home design, travel, and the Sunday magazine.

He arrived at the paper in 1944 as a copyboy after graduating from the City College of New York. He had served as a telegraph clerk, a news intern, a reporter, a culture writer, a drama critic, a city editor, and assistant managing editor. In the 1970s, when the paper was look-ing to attract a wider demographic, Gelb spearheaded the creation of five daily special sections: Sports (Monday), Science (Tuesday), Living (Wednesday), Home (Thursday), and Weekend (Friday). Not only were these enormously successful with readers and advertisers, but they also forged a template that was adopted by hundreds of newspapers nationwide.

In the vast pressure cooker of the *Times'* newsroom, he was an unflagging force of nature. Tall and rangy with thinning gray hair, he had a prominent nose, a reluctant smile (at least in the office), and an unwavering air of self-confidence. By his jittery demeanor you would think there was a joy buzzer on his seat, and he could never stay in one place for long. (He once told me that he slept only four hours a night, "no matter how late I go to bed.")

The man was a firehose of story ideas. There was no aspect of the human condition that did not intrigue him, and he could get as worked up over a feature on littering in the subway as he did when he edited the Pentagon Papers. In that sense he reminded me of Theodore Roosevelt, who was once described as "constitutionally incapable of indifference."

Every morning Gelb scuttled into the office, suit pockets stuffed with slips of paper on which were scribbled story ideas, many of which would soon grace the feature pages of the *Times*. And the ideas erupted all day long—some brilliant, some good, some arcane, some virtually undoable. In his repeated circumnavigations of the vast newsroom, Gelb never walked; he loped. Head erect, arms akimbo, and gaining velocity on the straightaways, he gave the impression that flight was imminent. Often, he was looking for a reporter upon whom he could scatter his editorial baubles. Sometimes, when an overtaxed reporter spotted Gelb approaching, he would pick up his phone and feign an important call. It rarely worked.

Gelb pushed his writers hard. If a story was of particular interest, he might edit the copy himself, sometimes sending the reporter back out for more interviewing. This could be exacerbating, but it always led to a better story. He pushed us to our limits and then some. And if you pulled off one of his quirky inspirations, or at least returned with scars indicating a good try, the praise was quick and genuine. Section editors, like Annette Grant (Weekend) and Alex Ward (Living), tell stories of Gelb ordering massive changes on deadline, or tearing up the entire section.

The portrait of Gelb that follows is lengthy, reflecting his outsized influence on my life.

"Hello, Bryan, take a seat; I'll be right with you," he said, seated at his paper-strewn desk. Hanging up the phone, he leaned forward, then closer, like a detective interrogating a cagey and unrepentant suspect. His phone rang and rang, making conversation impossible, so he suggested we head up to the executive dining room.

That had to be a good sign. The executive dining room, on the fourteenth floor, was the sanctum sanctorum of the company. Ninety percent of the laborers in the newsroom never saw its pale-yellow walls, crystal chandeliers, and long, gleaming oak table. The executive dining room was where editors hosted dignitaries, politicians, and sundry celebrities for informal, off-the-record interviews. It was a perfect venue for weighty conversation as its pallid, inert cuisine proved little distraction.

Right off the bat, Gelb went on the offensive: "So you know a lot about food? You are a good cook? Do you know French food? Can you make some of the classic sauces?"

It was going to be a long lunch.

"Uh, yes, I have made almost all of them," I lied.

"Good. There will be a lot of cooking in this job."

This was followed by, "What are some of your favorite restaurants in New York?"

Uh-oh.

Apart from my year at the Columbia University school of journalism, I had never lived as an adult in New York City. I was entirely unacquainted with the gastronomic landscape. In fact, I do not believe that I had frequented more than three "fine" establishments in Manhattan at that point, and those were of minor league caliber. Truth be told, my dining universe was largely circumscribed by Connecticut and Rhode Island, which, at the time, were hardly overpopulated with world-class culinarians.

The only well-known restaurant that came to mind was Lutèce. I had never set foot there, but it was widely hailed as the best restaurant in New York City, if not the nation. This I recall because, when at Columbia, a classmate named Rob asked me to recommend a romantic spot where he could woo a co-ed. I flipped through the phone book and perused the establishments that had paid for advertisements. It was not particularly useful. Stumped, I rang up a friend of my parents who worked on Wall Street.

"Lutèce," he declared confidently. "I think she'll swoon over that place."

"How much do you think it will cost?" Rob asked.

I suggested he bring a hundred dollars, just to be safe. That turned out to be far from safe; their gratuity included coins.

It turned out that Gelb was particularly enamored of Lutèce, and he ran on in sumptuous detail about how he and his wife, Barbara, had enjoyed an anniversary dinner there the previous year, and how André Soltner, the patron and chef, prepared a special dish of Alsatian-style lamb. What is more, dessert comprised frozen soufflés garnished with little red hearts of meringue. I never imagined that over the next decade I would dine at Lutèce more than twenty-five times, and assign it four stars on three occasions.

The rapturous anniversary meal at Lutèce brought to mind other memorable repasts Gelb had enjoyed over the years, and he related them in impressive detail. I listened politely, confirming his assessments with affirming nods. So far, I was scoring points while barely saying a word.

I told Gelb about my first acquaintance with Manhattan haute cuisine, in 1979, when a college classmate invited me to Le Veau d'Or, on East 60th Street, near Bloomingdale's. It was a revelation. Opened in 1938, it was a little patch of France on Manhattan's East Side: faded posters of the old country, black-and-white photos of the French countryside, smoked-stained ceiling, lipstick red banquettes, and lilting accordion music. And then there was the longtime patron, Monsieur Robert Tréboux, one of the legions of post-World War II French immigrants who arrived on ships, most of which docked in the West Fifties. Many of the culinarians went into the restaurant trade on those blocks, creating a marvelous little Frenchtown in the northern reaches of Hell's Kitchen. Sadly, virtually all of the bistros have disappeared, replaced by cold, unappetizing high rises.

A native of Haute Savoie, near the town of Evian, Mr. Tréboux came to America in 1952 and landed a job at a theatrical bistro called Maud Chez Elle, at 40 West 53rd Street, then moved over to the fabled Le Pavilion, at 5 East 55th Street, before striking out on his own with a partner to buy Le Close Normand and Le Manoir, both in Midtown.

Trim and talkative, he was in his late sixties when I first met him. Monsieur Robert (no one called him Monsieur Tréboux) affected dark suits, colorful vests, and energetic ties. He had a bright, impish smile, especially when ladies dropped in after exercising their credit cards at Bloomingdale's. Le Veau d'Or was moderately successful in those days, a haunt of homesick French expatriates and New Yorkers desirous of revisiting experiences they enjoyed on European vacations.

I perused the exotic sounding menu, which was penned in French, and asked my dining companion what tempted him.

"I love bouillabaisse," he said.

A well-dressed man at the next table was tucking into a crock of something that looked like baked beans with sausages.

"I'll get that," I declared.

Monsieur Robert, an avid partisan of Bordeaux wines, poured us two glasses.

"A votre sante Monsieurs!" he exhorted.

We sipped. It was fantastic, smooth, fruity, a little puckery, and with a long and pleasant finish. Monsieur Robert presented the bottle. It was a "Crus Bourgeois," Chateau de Pez. That designation indicates a quality wine although not in the more prestigious top tier.

Cassoulet was an eye opener. The earthy beans were enriched with shards of succulent pork combined with buttery preserved duck, called confit. Bouillabaisse, a celebrated seafood stew from Provence, was a faintly sweet, garlicky tomato-based broth holding morsels of fish and shellfish.

Ever refilling our glasses, Monsieur Robert suggested for dessert oeufs à la neige (floating islands), which I was familiar with, having made several times: poached clouds of meringue floating on *crème anglaise* (a thin custard sauce), followed by silken crème caramel.

I was straining to come up with other restaurant names to impress Gelb. He saved the day by running on about *his* favorite restaurants, two of which were Shun Lee Palace, a swanky Chinese place on the Upper West Side, and the Russian Tea Room, where he frequently supped with Broadway luminaries like Woody Allen and Jason Robards. Conversation returned to the *Times* and what a special place it was. Then he threw me a curve ball by noting that he had read my clips and that I "should work on making my writing a little more lively."

I was staggered by that remark. In the staid and cautious world of the *Times,* my writing was nothing short of stand-up comedy. Sometimes I was surprised at what I got away with. Maybe he was just trying to get a rise out of me. I searched for another topic about which Gelb could discourse. Did he have any changes in the works regarding the *Times'* food coverage? Surely that would eat ten minutes off the clock, as Gelb, to be sure, would have a million new ideas. I was aware that he needed to wrap up the interview by 2:45 p.m. in order to attend the daily front page editors' meeting. The final minutes of the Gelb interview were consumed by *New York Times* chest-thumping: "We are the greatest newspaper in the country and carry enormous responsibilities. You can be the most famous food writer in the country..." That sort of thing. Forsaking the canned fruit cocktails, we took our leave.

The meeting had gone as well as I could have hoped. Even so, my health was preeminent. Nothing else mattered. On the train to Westport, the winter sky was a chiaroscuro of blue, orange, and white. I deemed that a good omen for Anne and me. That evening Nancy Newhouse, the urbane editor of the Style Section, confirmed that, indeed, Gelb had come away with a positive impression.

The following day, I was informed by Gelb's secretary that Abe would be in contact. Excellent news, provided my health held up. Weeks passed with no word. Anything could be happening. I had experienced two depressive troughs since the Gelb lunch, bad ones. It was mid-January, and we were having a little French family reunion in our cottage: Anne's grandmother had flown over from France with her daughter, Isabel, who was Anne's age but technically her aunt, and her boyfriend, Peter. Anne's brother, Lionel, was living with us while studying English in the city. Being a Francophile, all of this was great, for it afforded me the opportunity to speak fifth-grade French with them.

I had never met Rosenthal, but felt as if I knew him because his fingerprints marked every facet of his splendid institution. Abe was the embodiment of the *Times* and, one might say, it of him. He ran the news department with Calvinist fervor, and those who abjured the scriptures suffered swift and lacerating wrath. To be sure, during his eight-year tenure as executive editor, the paper reached editorial heights equal to any in its hundred year existence.

On the appointed day, my depression, by my mood chart, was two days from lifting, so it was going to be tough, but doable.

Upon entering the *Times*, I felt dizzy and slightly nauseous, but, curiously, a little more lucid. On my one to ten mood chart—ten for feeling normal, one primed for autopsy—I was a solid eight, not good, but I could probably slog through it. My lips were as dry as fly paper. I felt I could look the part and answer straightforward questions but not much else. Days before the meeting I sought guidance from my editors on how to comport myself in the interview.

My first visit was at the desk of Alex Ward in the Living Section. A talented, likable editor, he was instrumental in bringing me into the paper and was the person for whom I had worked most closely for two years as a freelancer.

"Be lively and aggressive. Abe likes that," he advised.

"That I can do," I said.

I approached another veteran at the paper, Harold Gal. Amiable, fastidious, and a natty dresser, Gal functioned as the traffic cop of the section, keeping tabs on who was doing what. He was older than much of the staff and had done tours in various sections of the paper.

"Just be yourself," he said. "Don't try to wow him and be overly eager."

"Got it."

I approached Style editor Nancy Newhouse, who, as I have mentioned, was an erudite, exceedingly cultured New Yorker and one of the highest-ranking women at the paper.

"The most important thing," she said, "is that you be really upbeat and enthusiastic about the paper. Abe likes that."

"No problem."

Armed with the authoritative, if contradictory, advice, I entered the inner sanctum, where the careers of countless *Times* staffers have either taken off or crash-landed.

Rosenthal loved India, which he covered in the 1950s, and his office looked it, replete with Indian figurines, vibrantly colored fabrics, massive art books, and photographs. When I entered the room, he was slouched on a sofa, looking weary, as if I had caught him in mid-nap.

"Come on in," he beckoned.

"Good afternoon," I said, nervously.

"So, Nancy and the others think very highly of you."

"Thank you."

I estimated Rosenthal to be in his late fifties. With a gruff and skeptical demeanor, he epitomized my vision of a newspaperman. He wore dark, wrinkled suits, subdued ties, and rumpled white shirts. A colleague once described him as a "walking unmade bed." (Toward the end of his career he married a woman in the fashion business and underwent a startling sartorial makeover. I preferred the unmade bed.) Abe's temperamental weathervane could spin unpredictably, and most veterans on the paper knew when to duck.

"This isn't a formal interview, just a get together."

Well then, the heat's off. I exhaled. As it was merely a guys' tête-à-tête, I eased back into the deep couch, crossing my legs and stretching my arms behind my head. First mistake.

"You know," he said. "People who come to the *Times* don't leave the *Times*."

"I can understand that."

"I would be making a very big long-term investment in hiring you," he said, gazing toward the ceiling and calculating on his fingers. I gazed at the ceiling, too.

"Let's see, you are thirty, so let's say you stay thirty years ... that would come to, oh, nearly three million dollars."

How can one respond to that?

"I know everything about you. I've read everything you have written."

That I took as good news. He ventured that my work had been widely praised by editors and colleagues, even readers who had sent letters to the paper. My lively writing style, he said, laced with humor and satire, was something fresh and distinctive.

Following some small talk, mostly about India, he turned serious.

"If you were running the paper what changes would you make?"

Shit. He is hiring me to write about asparagus, what do I know about changes I would introduce on the foreign desk?

"Well, I would say, that, as far as I can tell, nothing in the short term."

I might as well have recommended placing potted forsythia around the foreign desk to liven things up. He clambered off the couch and shook my hand.

On the train home, satisfied with my overall performance, I bought two beers and pressed my head against the cool window. Finally, it was out of my hands. Anne was excited. We were on our way. I waited for the congratulatory phone call from Nancy for close to a week. Maybe they needed time to organize the welcome wagon office party. Finally, she called and asked if we could meet for lunch at an Italian restaurant that was across the street from the 21 Club.

"How did your session with Abe go?" she inquired.

"Great, great . . . very relaxed."

"Well," she said, "It did not go well at all. Abe thinks you lack energy and ambition and do not appear to be *Times'* material."

I nearly spit out my chardonnay. Abe had told Nancy that he was not blocking the hire nor was he recommending it. In other words, Nancy, who had spearheaded this process, would be assuming the risk. I told her not to put her neck on the line. It was okay. Remarkably, I was not terribly disappointed, but rather glad that the courtship had ended amicably. I could now start a new life, maybe at the *Boston Globe* or the *Baltimore Sun* or some such place. Besides, considering my mental condition, it was likely I would have lasted but a couple of months at the *Times* anyway.

Back in Westport, I discussed the developments with Anne. There were no hard feelings about the paper. The *Times* had been great to me, and I had learned a tremendous amount. Besides, I could still write articles for various sections. I wonder if I would have been so sanguine had I not been depressed. Depressed individuals—and I think I can speak for the vast majority of them—concern themselves with one thing: becoming un-depressed. Even today, I wear an emotional flak jacket that shields me from the tribulations of daily life. Aside from something happening to my son, Sean, nothing rattles me, not work, not finance, not smashing up my car. I simply say to myself, "at least I am not depressed." So I was perversely relieved to have my life's aspiration evaporate. For the time being, Anne and I would continue with our country life while pondering the next move. Or maybe move to France.

Two days later Nancy called. Before she could say anything I urged her again not to contravene Abe. I would be fine. She said she would call back the next day. By that time I had put the *Times* behind me and was happy to remain in Westport.

Nancy called the following day.

"Bryan, I have decided to go forward with the hire."

I poked my head out of the office and flashed a thumbs up to the French assembly.

All cheered.

CHAPTER 6
Panic in the Newsroom

ON FEBRUARY 7, 1983, A gray and glacial morning, I kissed Anne goodbye and boarded a shuttle bus to the Westport train station to embark upon my career at the *New York Times*, an event that, only two years before, seemed as improbable as assuming the chairmanship of General Motors. In the weeks building up to that historic day, my mood continued to swing—now it comprised a week of sprightly clarity followed by a week of immeasurable gloom. I arrived at the paper and paused at the revolving door. My hope was that the black bear would not follow inside. It did not. It entered first.

Slightly dizzy and muddled, I expected that my performance on the stage of world-class journalism would be fleeting. Even so, I managed a mini-celebration, a trifling one, but something I had dreamt about for a long time. In the past, whenever I entered the building, a security guard handed me a wall phone to call an editor for permission to enter. That little ritual underscored that I was simply work-for-hire, as dispensable as used copy paper. But that day was different. I reached into my shoulder bag and proudly retrieved a laminated name tag attached to a neck chain. It carried my photo and signature, and across the top, the words: "The New York Times." I had made it—a Navy Seal! Even though, my debut at the paper was hardly propitious. Like every *Times* conscript, I was subject to a six-month probation.

As a result of the disastrous interview with Rosenthal, I was probably considered a "C" student at best, unlikely to make it to Thanksgiving break. I would be under close and skeptical scrutiny by the top brass.

Stepping off of the elevator on the third floor, I gazed over the corporate topiary of the newsroom, all rust-orange and beige, with piles of newspapers and books everywhere. Intensely-focused reporters clicked at their keyboards; others, off deadline, sauntered around the newsroom with cups of coffee or read newspapers. I was a little surprised at the formality of the place. All men wore suits and ties. Female reporters donned what I suppose you could call business attire.

Until the mid-1970s, the *Times*' newsroom, on West 43rd Street, was a sprawling, messy, noisy, smoky, un-ergonomic, drably monochromatic word factory. Several of the old timers secreted bottles of alcohol in their desks, although I never witnessed imbibing on deadline. It was perfect. By the time I joined fulltime, it was very 1980s: an open layout with undersized cubicles, better lighting, wall to wall carpeting, no smoking, presumably little drinking, and a more relaxed sartorial manner. Men wore suits, although it was permissible to drape the jacket over the back of the chair.

Like every newspaper I had worked at, the *Times* was notably egalitarian as far as offices go. A stranger walking into the newsroom would not easily identify the big hats from the worker bees. A couple of the bosses had modest offices, but for the most part, they were on the front lines with everybody else.

It was a thrilling place to be. You could walk to the coffee cart and pass a couple of Pulitzer Prize winners or other journalistic dignitaries without even noticing. If you needed expert information on a particular topic, any topic—classical music, Canadian politics, fashion, the 1947 Brooklyn Dodgers—there was somebody nearby who was happy to edify you.

Most journalists—at least those who are not on a pistol-to-the-forehead deadline—enjoy being interrupted. They are grateful, actually. And, of course, they are natural storytellers. I enjoyed chatting with an unassuming man named Selwyn Raab, who covered organized crime. He was a repository of *Godfather*-like stories, and I looked forward to those involving shoot-outs and one-way excursions to the East River. We spoke about collaborating on a story about New York City restaurants where mobsters partook of their last earthly meals. He would describe the rub-out; I would rate the food. For whatever reason we never got around to it.

Standing on the rim of the newsroom on that first morning, I reasoned that, if I were to perish on my first day at work, it would be with pluck. Like a brazen foot soldier marching toward a phalanx of bayonets, I strode across the newsroom wearing a defiant grin. I could not escape the harsh irony that my desk was situated in a far corner of the newsroom, adjacent to the paper's enormous repository of clippings. In newspaper parlance it is called the morgue.

Naturally, as the new whiz kid on the block, editors expected me to come up with some stellar story proposals. After all, I could be siphoning three million dollars from the *Times* treasury, so it was understandable. In my sane and productive life, I was a wellspring of compelling ideas. It is said that a good journalist can parachute into any town and come out with an interesting story by sundown. That was me. I spotted stories behind every tree—offbeat, humorous, satirical, bizarre—which I suppose is why the paper had valued me as a freelancer. To have good ideas, asserted Linus Pawling, the Nobel Prize winning scientist, you have to have lots of ideas. At that moment, however, not a single inspiration came to mind.

An editor came by and dropped a press release on my desk concerning a demonstration of Colonial-era cooking, in Tarrytown, New York, a thirty minute ride up the Hudson River. Ordinarily, that kind of cushy feature would be a breeze, a day's work. On that morning, it felt like Watergate. I recall being in a rental car driven by a young woman photographer named Sarah Krulwich. She was no stranger, for we both broke into the business at a feisty little daily outside of Hartford, Connecticut, called the *Journal Inquirer*. She had been at the

Times for some years already, and had made quite a splash as a pioneering female in her field.

Details of the assignment have faded—something about women in bonnets cooking over a hearth—but one moment stands out with chilling clarity: Traveling north on the Saw Mill River Parkway, I had an urge to jump out of the car. That was the first time I had contemplated suicide, and although it was not close to actionable, it opened the door to a dark room that would both invite and repel me for years to come.

Contrary to conventional belief, many people who attempt to end their lives do not do so out of hopelessness, or lack of self-esteem, or personal loss, or even penury. They do it to stop the pain, emotional and physical, in the way a person trapped in a burning high rise will jump because the alternative is considered worse. On that day I fleetingly yearned for the grave. But I guess I had not yet played all of my cards.

The following morning, slowly, bluntly, I commenced a task for which I had been trained and had accomplished hundreds of times. Certain that my writing was worse than the text on a cereal box, I turned it in. It prompted no cackling from the copy desk—that was good—so I remained in my cubicle for the rest of the day. The next assignment was an Arthur Gelb special. Where do celebrities in the fine arts dine, where are their hangouts, what do they like to eat? I was not acquainted with any celebrities, much less their nocturnal lairs. I would have to wing it.

It is uncommon for a reporter to interview a reporter in order to report a story, but I was in a bind. My first stop was the office of Frank Rich, the paper's renowned theater critic. He could not have been nicer or more generous with his time. The first place he steered me to, naturally, was the celebrated Sardi's, on West 44th Street, where the cafeteria grade fare failed to discourage its Broadway regulars, many of whom are honored in caricatures that grace the walls.

Another theater hot spot was the casual pub-like Joe Allen's, on West 46th Street, and the venerable Algonquin, on West 44th Street. I must have visited twenty restaurants that regularly hosted art dealers, music producers, publishers, fashion executives, and more. It should have been an agreeable excursion around town. But I was depressed as hell. It was awful. Somehow I rallied to write, although it required twice as long to do so. It started like this:

If New York City is the nation's most prolific garden of theater, literature, fashion, and art, then certain restaurants here might be described as its fertile seedbeds, especially at lunchtime. At midday at any of these establishments—the Russian Tea Room, the Four Seasons, the Odeon, La Grenouille, and Les Pleiades are just a few of them—ideas are germinated, connections made and fees settled that result in new plays, books, clothes and exhibitions.

Writing a restaurant review or article when down was a punitive exercise, no matter how many times I attempted it. Blood might have been dripping from my eyeballs as I composed, and it was not Pulitzer quality, but I always managed to turn it in, and no one complained. Six years after leaving the *Times*, the paper was converting clippings from newsprint to digital. It sent me a box containing virtually every story I had written, hundreds of them going back to my freelance days in the early 1980s. As an experiment, I read twenty restaurant reviews to determine if I could recognize those written when depressed. It was not totally apparent. Some of the reviews were stylistically flat and lacking the fillips of humor I liked to insert, but none were *bad*. Reliving it was bad.

When I was healthy, writing a restaurant review was a four-hour task; when in a fog, it could be two days. I would thud out several paragraphs and then lay on the floor in front of the fireplace for half an hour, caressing my head and cursing the deity that inflicts such anguish on an innocent soul. Astoundingly, I never missed a deadline.

A salient question, and one I needed to keep asking myself, was: How can such a crippled wretch make life or death judgements about restaurants, which are people's livelihoods? Naturally, it weighed heavily, and I was forever reviewing myself. If I had felt for a minute that I was unable to perform my job at a high level, I would have resigned.

Over time I came to realize that depression can be like the Mafia—three-quarters intimidation. It spooks you into believing you are helpless, incapable of accomplishing even the most mundane tasks. It is not always true. Truth was that with tremendous effort I *could* conduct phone interviews; I *could* go out on assignments; I *could* even write. It's like the old line about watching a dog dance on its hind legs: It may not be done well, but you are impressed that it's done at all.

Gelb loved the story. One might think that such an early triumph would dial down the anxiety of my probationary status. It does not work that way. To a depressed person, nearly everything is scary. One of them is the telephone. Not the phone itself, of course, but what it represents: interaction with normal people, people who will soon catch on that you are only lightly tethered to the planet. Journalists talk on the phone all day long. And because of that state of mind, I was convinced that my telephone conversations would go largely misunderstood by others and instantly forgotten by me. When I was in a particularly bad way, the jingling phone was a signal to walk away from my desk.

Less than two months into the job, I was scanning old copies of the newspaper that were displayed on a counter near the executive offices. I felt a headache coming on fast. My heart was accelerating rapidly. I became short of breath. Presuming it was the result of excess coffee, I paced around the newsroom, breathing deeply, avoiding eye contact. It worsened. I leaned against a file cabinet, sweaty, hands trembling. Returning to my desk, it felt as if my heart was going to burst through the rib cage, and my brain was about to explode. I presumed the *Times* had some kind of medical facility, but I had no idea where it was. I collared a mail courier who directed me upstairs. In the elevator I fell to my knees.

In the medical office I stretched out on an examination table, groaning loudly.

"I think I'm having a heart attack," I huffed to a nurse.

"Your heart is racing," she said. "And your blood pressure is very high."

"This I know; what can it be?"

A doctor arrived and performed a perfunctory exam as I squirmed in distress.

My symptoms were not those of a heart attack, he said, and he handed me two tablets of the tranquilizer Xanax. Within fifteen minutes I began to recover. He called me into a small, book-lined office.

"You have had a panic attack," he explained.

"What's a panic attack?" I asked.

"It's extreme anxiety compressed into a particular moment," he explained. "The causes are not entirely clear."

Some confuse panic attacks, which often have no predictable triggers, with anxiety attacks, which are usually linked to events in the present or the result of angst about the future. My symptoms were typical of the former. They generally last less than fifteen minutes if untreated.

"Have you been feeling all right lately?" the doctor asked.

I let it all out, starting with the first day in Westport.

He listened patiently.

"I think you should consult with a psychiatrist," he advised, flipping through a file cabinet and removing a folder. He scribbled on a slip of paper and handed it to me.

"This is someone we have worked with in the past."

I returned to the newsroom, perplexed, angry, and frightened. Consulting a psychiatrist was a chilling thought. I used to joke that eleven out of ten women in Manhattan were in therapy, and that in most cases it was merely expensive handholding. No doubt that applied to men as well, although they are less prone to talk about it. In the 1980s, mental illness was said to be losing some of its stigma owing to media attention and the increased willingness of people to openly discuss it. I was not convinced. Apart from sympathetic bosses like Arthur Gelb, telling a supervisor that you suffered spells of depression was like confessing you are occasionally cruel to animals. In any case, settling onto a professional couch would make it official: I had joined the ranks of the broken.

As I returned to the newsroom, it was humming with normal people—actually, above normal people—engaged in what I loved to do but feared was coming to an end. On the way to my desk I stopped in the men's room, closed the stall door, took a seat, and wept.

CHAPTER 7
Shrinks

TRAMPING DOWN FIFTH AVENUE ON a damp, sullen afternoon, I headed to a psychiatrist I knew nothing about while suffering from a disease I did not understand in order to describe the indescribable. Arriving at a row of dignified nineteenth-century townhouses bordering Washington Square Park, in Greenwich Village, my first thought was: *this is going to be expensive.* I strolled along the block of handsome Federal and Greek revival architecture. Henry James lived in one of those houses. Edward Hopper painted in a little aerie way up there. Greeting me in the vestibule was a musty, professorial looking man with flocculent gray hair and a suspicious expression, as if I were about to hand him a Chinese menu. We retired to a small book-lined office in the back. No sooner had I settled onto a couch than I noticed a four-legged black streak darting through the door in my direction. At once I was under siege by a frenzied coil of black hair and sputum named Pete.

"Down, Pete!" commanded his owner. "How did you get in here boy?"

Pete moistened my wool trousers and pawed at my crotch before he was schussed out of the room. Most hosts would be appalled if their dog misbehaved like that, and would offer a million apologies.

"Pete likes you," the doctor said.

I recounted my life over the past year as he scribbled notes. At the conclusion, barely ten minutes, he made a few inquiries about my family history and said something I found objectionable.

"You have to understand," he intoned, "If I take you on, you must commit to remaining in treatment for a minimum of two years."

Two years? I was planning on a quick summer course, not a master's degree. He hardly knew me. Besides, how would such an agreement be enforced? Is that how psychiatry operates? I nodded in affirmation but did not mean it. Politely I took my departure as Pete expressed his displeasure by licking the front window.

Though I was behind on work, for the rest of the day I remained at home watching TV. The following morning I returned to the *Times'* medical office and informed the doctor that, no offense, but I was not keen on his recommendation.

Back to the file drawer.

"Do you have any problem with a woman?" he asked.

"I suppose not."

At work I entered a surprisingly productive streak, with only mild cycling. In six weeks I produced five stories that appeared on the cover of the Living Section. But my daily journal told the flip side.

July 3, 1984

Had three good days. Glorious. I wrote a long feature story in four hours. After the crash, a similar story would take two-and-half days. Last evening gave a speech to the Blair Summer School for Journalism (Blairstown, New Jersey). I was in such bad shape I lost track of my thoughts several times and had to start over. Skipped the cocktail party in my honor.

The following week I called upon a Dr. Katherine Falk at her home office on East 88th Street. In her late thirties, she was a pleasant if reserved woman, concise and confident. Dr. Falk wore large red eyeglasses and a thick sweater in the eighty-degree apartment.

I was angry and ashamed to be there, which was not the best attitude for launching a professionally intimate relationship. Like many individuals who are felled by depression, I carried a large measure of guilt. A broken arm has a clear cause and effect, and a remedy. You have an idea of when it will heal. Friends can sign your cast. A broken mind is indefinable, almost spectral. One thing that makes depression so insidious is that the tool required to fix the disease (the brain) is the brain itself—it's like fixing a flat tire with a flat tire. Moreover, when people see you suffering for no apparent reason, it's natural to assume the problem is "in your head." And if the problem is in your head, you must have done something to precipitate it. And if you did something to precipitate it, it should be within your powers to fix it. The worst thing you can say to a depressed person is "buck up," or "pull yourself out of it." The best one can do is to be available and vigilant.

Dr. Falk was a fine psychiatrist, although my skeptical attitude, at least for the first six months, at times found us at odds. Early on, she confidently diagnosed my illness as a "garden variety depression," which I likened to a "run-of-the-mill lung transplant." It was heartening when she added, "I have never treated a depression like yours that I could not cure." I wanted to leap across the desk and kiss her.

Psychiatrists invariably begin treatment by inquiring if depression runs in the family. As a measure of how benighted I was about psychotherapy, that question appeared pat and irrelevant. I needed help *then* and had no time for history lessons. Besides, I really could not contribute much. Virtually all of my male forbears left the playing field early, with scant testament to any earthly triumphs. A number of their siblings and spouses outlived them, some by decades, yet I did not think of interviewing them until I commenced this book, by which time it was fairly late in the game. I noted that my father died when I was only three years old—he was twenty-five—and that that was pretty much all I knew. I was too young to have meaningful memories. She didn't buy that.

In the ensuing months, Dr. Falk maneuvered her therapeutic backhoe over my landscape of anxieties. Ever so gradually, I came to understand that not only did I remember a great deal more than I had believed, but also that escape from my demons would only come once I exposed them, dragged them into the sunlight, and spit in their faces. Clearly, my father's death, and the events surrounding it, was a hydrogen bomb on a thirty-year timer. But it was not so simple, as we shall see.

In the course of my illness I nibbled from a Whitman's Sampler of pharmaceuticals. At times I was gagging down well over a hundred pills a week—a walking Duane Reade: Tofranil, Nortriptyline, Lithium, Wellbutrin, Nardil, Depakote, Zyprexa, Ativan, Effexor, Levothyroxine, Prozac, Xanax, and others. Some of them offered relief for a short time and then failed. And most of these medications require boundless patience as they can take six weeks or more to reach therapeutic blood levels, an agonizing wait. Imagine taking a Tylenol for a throbbing headache and having to wait half a college semester to feel better. And you cannot simply stop taking one antidepressant and start with another. Often you must wait a week or more for the first one to wash out of your system. It can be hell.

My experience was not uncommon. Drug treatment for depression is a bit of a roulette wheel. Two-thirds of people do not respond to the first medication. As many as a third do not respond to several. Then there are those like me who fall into the waste bin labeled TRD, or treatment resistant depression, generally defined as four or more failed attempts. Researching psychotropic medications I came up with some startling facts. Studies involving adults with moderate to severe depression show the following:

- Of those who took antidepressants, about forty to sixty out of a hundred noticed improvement in their symptoms within six to eight weeks.
- Of those who took placebos, about twenty to forty out of a hundred notice improvements in their symptoms within six to eight weeks.

Go figure.

With the drugs yielding mixed results, Dr. Falk had another path to explore. Environmental factors have been known to provoke depression and other reactions. The following week I drove out to an allergist in Madison, New Jersey. A friendly and enthusiastic fellow, he pricked my arm with more than a dozen allergens including common household molds and a number of foods. If I developed a rash over any of the prick marks he would investigate further. In fifteen minutes he examined the arm and said that I might be allergic to one or two of the molds. As a follow-up, he presented me with a little box that held vials of liquefied molds along with hypodermic needles the length of chopsticks, or so they seemed. I was to inject myself in the thigh, daily, for five days. *Do what?*

It was not as painful as it sounded. Meanwhile, at home, I brandished a flashlight and foraged throughout the house in search of these "common household molds," despite having no idea what they looked like. In the end, it turned out that I suffered no allergies to molds or anything else.

It was time for Dr. Falk to call in a designated hitter, a psychiatrist whom she described as "the best diagnostician I have ever known." His name eludes me now, but he was tall and brash, an in-your-face sort of guy. I took an immediate dislike to him and, unwisely, was minimally cooperative. He scared the hell out of me talking about hospitalization and worst case scenarios, and thousands of dollars in fees for sundry treatments. My lack of enthusiasm was conveyed to Dr. Falk, who rightly chastised me about wasting everybody's time.

In late 1985, my affliction was still new enough to allow for hope and old enough to distrust it. I continued expensive (for me) biweekly visits to Dr. Falk, who continued to reassure me that before long I would be the live wire of the *Times*' newsroom. Nonetheless, these were among the darkest days in my life. One minor image shadows me still. Every time I descended to Dr. Falk's elegant lobby, I attempted to steal out unnoticed. At the entrance stood a jaunty Irish doorman who, upon spotting me, would chirp:

"You have a sunny day, young fella'!"

Often I knew I was not going to have a sunny day. I don't know why that rattled me so, but it did.

Dr. Falk decided to bring in reinforcements on the pharmaceutical front. She bundled me up and dropped me at the doorstep of one Dr. Michael R. Liebowitz, a nationally renowned psychopharmacologist at Columbia University's Psychiatric Institute. He was (is) considered the Yo Yo Ma of the biochemical set. When other doctors hit the wall with intractable patients, they often sent them his way.

Among Dr. Liebowitz's many accomplishments was creating the country's first anxiety disorders clinic, in the 1970s. I was equally impressed by the fact that, in 1983, he published a book about the physiological changes that take place in the body when one falls in love, called *The Chemistry of Love.*

I met Dr. Liebowitz on a blustery fall evening when I was so sick I had not been out of the apartment for two days. My brain was pounding; I wanted to slug somebody. Anne was in Westport, and I requested she stay there until things settled down. She was already distraught about my behavior, and I did not want her to see me in this condition. The appointment was in a small, windowless office in a building called the Eye Institute, three blocks from the towering New York State Psychiatric Institute.

Dr. Liebowitz is a rangy, taciturn man with a soft voice and parenthetic mustache. When he speaks it is as if he is looking through you and directly at your disease. You do not necessarily visit him for an exegesis of your problem—at least I did not—you visit him to get better, fast.

He interviewed me in a deliberate and dispassionate manner, and then went silent. He gazed at the ceiling. As I came to learn, that was a good sign; his hard drive was spinning. He revised my drug regimen and asked me to return in two weeks. Two weeks is an eternity to depressed individuals; but as I have explained, many antidepressants require four weeks or more to kick in.

I continued researching depression and learned something both surprising and unsettling. Between 20 percent or more of people taking antidepressants quit within the first three months, even if they have substantially recovered, citing unpleasant side effects. Those taking lithium in particular may complain of feeling "dull" and "sluggish" and with diminished "creativity." Others simply do not like the idea of taking long-term medications. I have spoken with a number of these people in depression help groups, and have tried to persuade them that ditching meds prematurely because they make you feel logy is like ignoring your rip cord because the parachute blocks the view.

Around that time Anne said that she would like to speak with Dr. Falk. I was surprised but felt it might be helpful. I would not be in the room. At my following session, Dr. Falk recounted, with permission, that Anne was terrified, and angry about our situation, which seemed to be getting worse. Anne told her that she had already lost a loved one to mental instability and feared I would be next. I imagine Dr. Falk tried to comfort Anne with the "garden variety" comparison. There was not much I could say other than that I was tilling as fast as I could.

By that time it was all but certain that my father's death was the central issue in my deterioration some thirty years after the fact. And I was engaged in a two-front war, biochemical and emotional. Which of these caused the other was not clear, and I suppose it did not really matter. Dr. Falk homed in on my mother's response to that horrific event in 1955 and how it impacted me. It always starts with the mother.

Chapter 8
Latchkey Girl

EVERYONE SAID MY MOTHER, DOROTHY, looked like Doris Day. And she did. In the sixties there was a forgettable sitcom called *The Doris Day Show*. I watched it only to see Dorothy fall into humorous family predicaments. And like Doris, she loved to sing. All she needed were the lyrics to "Sera Sera" and she could have made a fortune in Las Vegas as a Doris Day impersonator.

One could not have asked for a more entertaining parent, which was unlikely considering her difficult upbringing. She possessed an endless repository of jokes—not all fitting for genteel company—and a practiced prankster; my younger sister, Diane, and I were mortified when she danced in the supermarket aisles. Familiar to a fault, she was always hugging and kissing people she barely knew.

"Who was that, mom?" I would ask.

"I don't know, I think I met her at a party somewhere."

If there was a melancholy undertow to her fun-loving ways, I did not pick up on it. Diane did, and she ventured that our mother was compensating for something dark.

Dorothy spent part of her childhood in the safe and sociable Norwood section of the north Bronx, a mostly Irish, Italian, and Jewish neighborhood. Her parents divorced when she was a pre-teen and, regrettably, that is more or less the extent of my knowledge about those years. Grandma Dot, a striking fashion plate out of the roaring twenties, worked as a telephone operator at a Manhattan publishing house. She sat along with several co-workers in front of a marvelous black wall of telephone jacks and cords and buzzers and little flashing lights. Unfortunately for young Dorothy, Grandma Dot never warmed up to the child rearing profession, favoring the bright lights of Manhattan and the Bronx—yes, the Bronx once had a spirited nightlife. In the post-war years the northern Bronx, particularly Norwood and Woodlawn, was so safe, a contemporary told me, that he parked his convertible on the street overnight, top down, without concern. After the divorce, my mother was sent to live with her father in Yonkers.

George Hayden survives in three small, faded photographs that I display on my living room bookshelf. When I look at these it is hard to believe that someone who seems as distant as the pharaohs could have, health permitting, lived into my teen years and been a real grandfather. He was a tall and handsome German, with deep-set eyes, finely etched features, and a thicket of black hair. I am told I inherited his looks however I do not detect it. For most of his working life he was in the employ of the Otis Elevator Company, among the largest industries in Yonkers at the time. Its founder, Elisha Otis, gained renown by inventing the "safety elevator" in the 1850s. This most welcome innovation was a braking system to catch runaway cars from plummeting to the ground, leaving passengers six inches shorter than when they entered.

My mother said that the days with her father were happy and loving. I have photos of her dressed for Easter, playing with her little black dog, going to school, and waiting at a bus stop. When she was fourteen, she began to notice changes in her normally vibrant father. At first he developed a hand tremor. It worsened to the point that he could not hold a coffee cup without spilling its contents. Over the following months his arms and legs weakened. His face drooped, making it difficult to eat. The diagnosis was myasthenia gravis, a neuromuscular disease that causes skeletal-muscle weakness among other symptoms. This is the result of a failure of communication between nerves and muscles. At the time, it was an assassin. Today, with modern medications, those with mild cases can live a functional, independent life. There remains no cure. George Hayden, single father, elevator worker, passed away at age forty-nine.

Dorothy was shipped off to her father's sisters in Hudson, New York, a former river port a hundred miles north of Yonkers. Neither was in the market for a teenage girl but under the circumstances they grudgingly acquiesced. From what I can tell from two photos they lived in a big farmhouse on what looked like an orchard. My mother likened her nearly two years upstate to living in an impersonal boarding house. About a year later, having overstayed her welcome, she was shipped back to an unreceptive Grandma Dot. Like Grandma Dot, Dorothy was a real looker, long-limbed, lively eyes, and black hair with her trademark bangs.

Back in the city, Dorothy was presented with a neck chain holding a latchkey for coming and going when her mother was in absentia, which was often. She attended nearby Evander Childs High School, a block-long pile of ocher bricks on Gun Hill Road. Unfettered by parental supervision, she passed many diverting school days at the magnificent Loew's Paradise movie house on the Grand Concourse. The five-mile-long Concourse, which bifurcates the Bronx from north to south, was six lanes wide and cushioned by a lush tree-lined median strip. It was dubbed, with a bit of New York bluster, as the "Champs-Elysees of the Bronx."

You do not need to know this, but I was curious about something: who was the gentleman behind the school's dignified name—a Civil War general? A World War I diplomat? A scientist? I discovered that Evander Childs was a mild mannered principal of another Bronx high school. Before classes one morning, in 1912, he was seated at his desk reading mail. As it was reported in the *New York Times*, the morning assembly bell sounded, startling Mr. Childs and causing him to fall and hit his head on the desk, with fatal consequences. It was likely the only time the New York City Board of Education named a high school after an accident.

The miniscule one bedroom apartment Dorothy shared with Grandma Dot was in one of those drab but not rundown six-story buildings with sunless courtyards that populate much of the borough still today. This was the turn of the 1960s, when living in a shoebox was more tolerable because the world outside of your door was calm and familiar, an extension of your living room. But things began to change. The first great wave of Bronx immigration was Hispanic, primarily from Puerto Rico, up to a million immigrants by 1965, and every one of them moved onto my grandmother's block. The noise and aromas and music and automobiles scared the bejesus out of Grandma Dot and her sister, Aunt Florie.

Aunt Florie was a roomy, pious woman, one of those individuals you cannot imagine ever having been young. For years, she lived in a sauna disguised as an apartment on the sixth floor of Grandma Dot's building. The widows in my family were discreet regarding their stricken husbands, so I have little intelligence concerning their lives. In fact, Grandma Dot never mentioned George Hayden's name, ever; Aunt Florie made passing reference to her husband Ricky, as skinny as a scarecrow under his rakish straw boater. Were the memories too painful? Did they feel that their lives were inconsequential? My belief is simple: nobody ever asked. And I kick myself for not doing so. As a teenager I spent many hours with them, chatting about school and sports while peeling off clothing and frequently rehydrating. But being a self-absorbed teen, I had few interests aside from my own stimulating life. I suppose that at that stage in life it appears that family members will be around for a long time. Grandma Dot was felled by cancer in her early seventies; Aunt Florie survived a few lonely years longer. They passed along dozens of photos but little family history. I have asked my son, Sean, to be a better historian than I.

Chapter 9
Skippy

MY MOTHER ALMOST NEVER SPOKE about my father, Albert J. Miller, known to all as "Skippy." Much of what I absorbed came from a handful of relatives and two of his now-deceased closest friends. Bright, popular, and embarrassingly good looking, he passed through my life like a shooting star. Skippy attended Manhattan Prep, in the Riverdale section of the Bronx, where he was senior class president, followed by Manhattan College, where he studied engineering. He had one older sister, Elaine.

My father completed a two-year hitch in the Air Force—I have lots of old Polaroid photos of him posing in front of airplanes—but I have no idea what he did, nor if he ever soared like an eagle. How my parents met is equally unclear. Dorothy lived less than a mile and a world away from Skippy—he a preppie Irish kid, she a public school student literally from the other side of the (subway) tracks. I have a wonderful photo of them at Skippy's high school senior prom. My mother had undergone oral surgery that day and looks as if she has an orange in her cheek.

Before we explored my father's life, Dr. Falk asked for details about his mother, my grandmother, Lina Miller, and whether she might have been touched by depression. I said that if I had to choose a least likely forbear to have been so afflicted it would be her. Then again, depressed people can be like vaudevillians—jovial and entertaining on stage, depleted and downcast in the privacy of the dressing room. Lina Miller was of medium height and weight, with pale, veined, Irish skin, and a finely chiseled nose. For the final twenty years of her nursing career she worked the nightshift, 4:00 p.m. to midnight, at a convalescent facility that was within walking distance from her one-bedroom apartment on McLain Avenue, on the Bronx-Yonkers line. Enjoying the benefits of two square meals at work, her solitary victualing at home was as spare as it was predictable: a bottle—make that many bottles—of Rheingold lager (at the time a popular Brooklyn-made brew) accompanied by a generous buffet of Tareyton 100's cigarettes. Diane and I observed that Lina inhaled but never seemed to exhale, and that one day she might lift off like a party balloon.

When her children were growing up she had a small cottage on Bainbridge in the Bronx that served as a youth clubhouse.

"She always had a keg of beer on tap," recalled my mother. "I don't remember any food. But there was a lot of singing and dancing. Your father played the piano by ear."

Diane and I spent a good deal of time with our grandmother. In the McClain Avenue apartment, one entered through a narrow hallway, and at the end of that hallway was a secretary desk that held two eight-by-ten photos, one of Skippy, the other of his sister, Elaine. To the right was my parents' formal wedding portrait. I remember how, on more than one occasion, when my mother was coming to retrieve us, Lina would ask me to hide the wedding picture in a drawer.

"It will make her sad," Lina said.

Many food writers rapturously recall how they developed a love for cooking at their grandmother's apron. I do not believe my grandmother even owned an apron. Nor did we ever sit down to a home-made meal at her place. Much of our dining took place at a coffee shop on the corner called the "Sit and Chat," where I favored the nickel-thin grilled cheese sandwiches and foamy milkshakes.

When I was about six years old, Diane and I often walked three blocks to her apartment for a sleep-over. We played Chinese checkers, a popular board game that has gone the way of the Slinky, and sang the Irish drinking ditty "Little Brown Jug." Lina had a small, underutilized kitchen that looked out over a dark alley. She found little use for the stout refrigerator save as a beer cooler. And the white enameled gas range, unsullied by contact with food, could have been returned to the appliance store and resold as new. Nonetheless, these visits were delectable occasions, for we could partake in one of our grandmother's culinary tours-de-force: Franco-American spaghetti, served in the can. Cold.

My favorite Lina story concerns the time she had my mother and Skippy over for dinner—meatloaf night. While preparing the ground beef, she reached up to a shelf to retrieve breadcrumbs but instead grabbed a box of Rinso, a soap powder.

"Mom," my father exclaimed upon taking his first bite. "This meatloaf tastes like soap."

"Tastes fine to me," she replied, and continued eating.

While in the military, after several months of eating GI chow, Skippy wrote to my mother, "Everybody here complains about the food. I don't understand it—this is the best food I've ever had!"

My grandmother alluded to her son every once in a while, but not in a particularly emotive way, at least not in front of us. She was more proud than sentimental. There is one detail that I carried around for a very long time, even today. One evening—it might have been in the course of a can opener repast—Lina informed me that my father, an engineer, was involved in the construction of an airplane hangar at LaGuardia airport, and that his name was on it. To a second-grader, that was an accomplishment of immense esteem. I had no clear idea of what an airplane hangar was, nor an engineer, but no matter, it was heroic, even if he drove the cement truck. To be honest, I would like to see that hangar if it still exists.

One evening, I think I was five, Lina came over to babysit overnight. As we had only two bedrooms, she slept in my room on a twin bed. I seized the opportunity to ask something that had obviously been on my mind for some time.

"Where is my father?"

"Well," she explained, "God loved him so much that he wanted to be with him early."

That seemed like a plausible scenario and remained a great source of comfort for some time. It was but a crumb of information, yet in the great emptiness surrounding his death, my imagination embellished it into an expansive feast.

Studies attest that toddlers and preschoolers may be too young to understand death, but they comprehend absence. They are totally dependent upon their parents, physically and emotionally. For them, the death of a parent has such a shattering effect on their sense of personal security that it is almost impossible to know the extent of its long-term damage. Young children lack the ability to process the actions and emotions of others. They cannot communicate adequately, which only exacerbates the fear. And it is without doubt that losing a parent at a very young age is the single most powerful cause of depressive illness, suicide, and later marital breakups.

Lacking the ability to comprehend the calamity playing out around them, young children begin to believe that they are culpable. That is a massive crucible to shoulder, and it can continue for decades. And if something like that happened once, they fear, it could easily happen again.

My mother recalled that for weeks after my father's death I padded around the apartment looking for him—out the window, in the bedroom, in the coat closet. I continually asked when he was coming home; when there was a knock on the door I scampered to open it. Periodically I stopped speaking for hours, or just stared at the television.

Children are often described as "resilient" and fast healers because, temperamentally, they appear to be "back to normal" in a fairly short time. Similarly, the surviving parent may return to a familiar routine, often out of necessity. I imagine that within months I stopped searching the house and resumed my four-year-old career. The damage was invisible, but indelible—for thirty years.

Following Skippy's hitch in the service, my parents married and settled on Duncan Street, in the little-known Olinville section of the Bronx, not far from the Bronx Zoo. A neat middle class enclave, it had wide streets, abundant foliage, and rows of two-story brick townhouses fronted by white metal canopies. My father was employed as an electrical engineer at the Port Authority of New York, while my mother, for the first time in her life, huddled under the lee of love and security. Judging from old photographs, they had a typical post-war couple's life: picnics at Jones Beach, taking their toddler to the park, family gatherings, and day trips upstate.

I have but one enduring image of my father, and I am certain it is true. I am sitting on the living room floor, and he is holding an overcoat on one arm and carries a small suitcase. He waves and says "goodbye, Bryan." He was on his way to the hospital, I am sure of it. And I remember many times when I worried a similar fate could befall my mother.

In mid-1956, Skippy developed a weakness in his arms and legs, similar to George Hayden. This was followed by debilitating fatigue. When it worsened he had an evaluation. Doctors were puzzled, but in time they confirmed it was lupus, an autoimmune disease that causes the immune system to attack healthy tissues and ultimately vital organs. There was no cure. Nor is there one today, but modern medications vastly reduce the symptoms.

Skippy was pumped up with drugs that added twenty-five pounds to his failing frame. I have a photo of him at that time, and he is unrecognizable. In early December, he was hospitalized. It is almost certain that my protective mother did not bring me to see him. I believe I was sent to a great aunt in Stamford, Connecticut.

"He was sick, but I had no idea he was going to die," my mother recalled. Fifteen days before Christmas he slipped away, in his twenty-fifth year. My mother was five months pregnant. She had lost the two most important men in her life—Skippy and her father, to an autoimmune syndrome.

It was heartbreaking when she recalled to me: "I was lost," she said. "All of these people around, all of these decisions. I was twenty-two years old—what did I know about buying a casket?"

Skippy's best friend, Al Franklin, purchased the casket, and chose the headstone. After the internment, Al and his brother, Ed, were determined to give me a real Christmas. I remember receiving a toy helicopter that was attached to a revolving base and spun around and around like a carnival ride. Photos show numerous wrapped boxes, but I have no recollections aside from the helicopter. I cannot imagine what my mother was going through.

It has been observed that young children who lose a parent tend to inflate that parent's qualities. I have always wondered how I would be different had I been raised by my real father. I am told that Skippy was a reader, and that he possessed an easy sense of humor. They say he was kind and generous. One day while visiting home from college, I was rummaging around in the small attic of our house looking for a suitcase and came across a box holding about twenty books by the *New Yorker* magazine humorist Robert Benchley, dating to the 1930s and 1940s. How did *they* get there? Had my mother lugged them from one residence to another? And why? Some were damp and even moldy. Nonetheless, that was an extraordinary discovery, one of the few intellectual tendrils that bonded me with my father—who, of course, was a genius.

I carried those books around for thirty years, one attic at a time. Every so often I would browse through one of the less sodden editions, but I found Benchley's humor dated and mannered. Still, I liked to picture my father lying on a couch, a beer on the side table, reading them and chortling. I hauled them around until the stench surpassed sentimentality.

Some months after Diane was born, our landlord paid a neighborly visit to inform us that he was not renewing the lease. The reason: He was concerned that a young widow with two children would not be able to carry the rent. We were living on my father's military pension at the time, just scraping by. I don't know how my mother did it, but she moved us to a much nicer place, a ground floor apartment with a patio in the thoroughly Irish enclave of Woodlawn. It was a block from the vast and verdant Van Cortlandt Park, perfect for children. Every Irish Catholic family in the neighborhood had thirteen kids, or so it seemed, so we never lacked for recreational opportunities. So many youngsters showed up for my fifth birthday party, on May 17, that folding tables spilled outside onto the patio. There were three cakes, and so many presents I was opening boxes until Memorial Day. And someone was always having a birthday party, so we were instructed to save our hats and noisemakers.

It was in the Woodlawn apartment that something transpired that was so emotionally profound that it stayed with me for life. And it represents the most important event that propelled my two-decade depression. My mother was sitting at a desk, paying bills—how I knew that is unclear, but I knew. She was crying. I approached her and said, reassuringly, "Don't worry mom, I'll take care of you." That was an astounding display of maturity for a three-year-old. At that moment I transformed from little boy to little husband, with all the responsibilities and hazards thereof. It forged a profound and complex bond with my mother, an emotional cinder block that I dragged around for decades.

My actions that day went beyond uncommon maturity—there was utter fear. As I note elsewhere, a very young child comprehends neither death nor causality. Thus at the time I believed that I had something to do with my father's disappearance, which is an overwhelming guilt for any child to carry.

At the same time my newborn sister was placing more demands on my mother. In my mind, that was breaking our sacred trust—it was supposed to be just the two of us. It was infuriating. To say that I developed a love/hate relationship with women later in life might be overstating it, but not by much.

The old apartment is still there, only twenty minutes from my home in Westchester County, and a dozen times I have stood outside or strolled around the neighborhood wishing for an opportunity to enter. For two years it was vacant and seedy looking. Today it is occupied, judging by the air conditioner in one of the windows. As badly as I want to go inside it, I hesitate to ring the doorbell. Who in these distrustful times would invite into their home a strange man with a sentimental family pitch? So I linger on the block in the event someone surfaces.

Genuine corroboration for what I call the checkbook scene did not come until my college years. My mother was hosting a casual dinner party in our large country kitchen while I sat nearby reading in the living room. At one point I heard her say, "... and I was crying, and Bryan, just a little boy, came over and said 'I'll take care of you, mom.'" What? One of the defining moments of my life, and I learn second hand via the neighbors? So typical of my mother. Evoking the episode with *me* could have brought it back to life, like a zombie climbing out of the grave. My intention was to bring it up the following day at breakfast when we were alone, but I changed my mind. Whatever prompted her uncharacteristic moment of candor—perhaps a third pinot grigio—it was never repeated, nor did I ask.

I mentioned to Dr. Falk that if there was a leading candidate for depression in the family it could be the hermetic Grandpa Miller, whom I had encountered but three times, the first two at ages five and seven (my best estimate). Albert J. Miller Sr. was employed by the United States Postal Service, doing what is not certain. My mother said he was of a bright scientific and mechanical mind, and could disassemble and put back together all kinds of machines, from car engines to fine watches. Grandpa Miller was devastated by his son's passing, which is understandable. Some years afterwards, he inexplicably left Lina, decamping to Brooklyn. No one ever explained what happened. He was just gone, although I was told that he appeared occasionally at family functions. Both Catholics, they never divorced.

Just as well, as far as my mother was concerned, for she found his woeful, weepy presence unbearable.

"Every time I saw him, he broke down crying about his son," my mother recalled. "I couldn't take it anymore, and I never saw him again."

When I was a junior in high school and my sister, Diane, a freshman, I decided to see if he had come to peace with his demons, and ascertain why he had snubbed his family for so long. One of my cousins had his phone number so I rang him up.

He appeared surprised, but not in the effusive way one would expect under the circumstances. He invited us to meet him at a friend's jewelry store on Canal Street, in Manhattan's Chinatown.

That was my first unescorted visit to Manhattan, and I had little idea where Chinatown was located. Exiting the Port Authority bus station we beheld a raucous and colorful scene. People swarmed up and down Eighth Avenue like bees in the summer heat; there were storefront pizza parlors, bodegas with fruit displayed on the sidewalk, smoke shops, liquor stores, and electronic stores the width of a bowling lane. Movie marquees announced round-the-clock carnal gratification.

We nervously flagged a cab and lurched down to Canal Street, close to the Manhattan Bridge. I knocked on a locked glass door. The ancient shop owner, who was not Chinese, ushered us in. On the far side of the room stooped Albert J. Miller Sr., studying a watch. He glanced up, inquisitively, as if we might be two random kids out for a walk.

Heavyset, with a large balding head, droopy visage, and unlively eyes, Grandpa Miller appeared sad even when he was not sad. Once we were safely identified, he shuffled over and hugged us. It was not a squishy moment, no warm surge of emotions. It was the kind of hug one might give the winner of a spelling bee. What could he be feeling? Joy? Guilt? Bemusement?

"Let's go to my friend's restaurant," he said.

We claimed a table in the crowded, harshly lit dining room of a Chinese restaurant. I strained to detect any family resemblance, but it was not evident with his hangdog mien and sleepy demeanor. He inquired about school, our hobbies, where we lived. He briefly asked about my mother. His son never came up.

He appeared a bit uneasy, tapping chopsticks against his water glass. As I remember, there was talk about his home in Brooklyn. As he spoke, my curiosity drifted in the direction of anger. How could he just walk away from his family, whether out of grief or some other reason? And even if he had a compelling motive to relocate, a Christmas card would have been nice. Maybe he had suffered from depression, I suggested to Dr. Falk. Like so many of the tormented, he wanted to be alone.

Our conversation was unmemorable. Yet, after time, I sensed from his body language and his tear-glistened eyes that it just might have been one of the most wonderful days of his life. But he left it at that— no invitation to his house someday, no arrangements to meet again. Was that too much for him to handle?

We read aloud our fortune cookies and walked back to the store. As we were about to depart, he led me behind a jewelry counter and opened a drawer to retrieve something made of dark leather.

"Here, Bryan," he whispered. "This is your father's wallet. You should have it."

Grandpa Miller did not cry.

I did.

CHAPTER 10
Hard Knocks

I WRITE THIS CHAPTER BECAUSE it shines a light on the years leading up to the depression. It is also a sketch of the man who, for better or worse, was my second father for nearly three decades. His contributions to my subsequent adult miseries are unclear; I believe that table was already set well before he came along.

My life shifted dramatically when we were living in the Van Cortlandt Park apartment. This strange and un-emotive man entered our lives. My earliest impressions, at age six, are indistinct, but right off I sensed he was not all that enamored of kids. He began showing up more often but was for the most part distant and indifferent. Baby-sitters entered our lives as he and my mother dated. The next thing I knew we were spending the summer at a damp, chilly log cabin high above a lake in New Jersey. Before I knew it, he was around all the time—my step-father. It may seem hard to believe, but my mother never told me that they had married, and I did not ask for some years.

Ben Butkus was a hot-tempered martinet and an Olympian drinker, hardly the nurturing role model I so desperately needed. He was a crazy, impulsive second-generation-Lithuanian who happened to have had another family, with four children, in Rhode Island. Ben carried much guilt about not being there for them. Some of them spent summers at Lake Lenape with us. As in many families with children by different parents, there was occasional tension about alleged favoritism on one side or the other. Ben conceded that he was tougher on me and Diane than on the others, and that he had set the bar higher for us because he recognized our potential.

Ben's oldest child, David, was bright and intense, someone to whom laughter came sparingly. It was evident, at least to me, that something dark smoldered within. After a brief stint in college he bounced around Rhode Island, eventually enlisting in the service, the Army I believe, and was sent to Korea. He was discharged under uncertain circumstances; he later married and had two children, girls, but it was short-lived. It was evident that David needed help, and he was not getting it. I aired this to my mother, and she had a word with Ben. I believe he spoke with David but nothing came of it. I lost touch with David for a number of years while feeling that I should have intervened. That was in the 1980s, and my depression was in full bloom. One day my mother called to say that David had shot himself in the head.

Ben was from hard-coal country in Eastern Pennsylvania, where his alcoholic father toiled in the mines until black lung took him out. Ben had to abandon elementary school to help support the family by collecting chunks of coal that fell off trains and onto the tracks. He was angry about that for the rest of his life. He was an intelligent and relatively well-spoken man, and in his early forties started his own trucking company, in Andover, New Jersey, near Lake Lenape. I have never doubted that my mother married him for our financial security, although like everything else, we never talked about it. She deserved so much better.

Soon after their furtive nuptials, in 1959 we moved from Woodlawn to the lake and settled in a two-bedroom ranch house with sweeping views and a long wood dock. At the time I was unaware of what Ben did during his workdays, although it always left him in a foul mood upon returning home. As a result, I believed that adult work was something onerous and disagreeable. You showed up, endured a dismal day, and returned home, infuriated about something. When Diane and I heard his car arriving, we would pretend to be doing our homework, or dash into the little bedroom we shared. Ben did not abide idleness. His philosophy of child rearing was as archaic as it was maddening: kids get a free ride in life—food, shelter, clothing—and as such have an obligation to reimburse the banker (him), usually with pointless manual labor. (Plucking weeds from a forested section of the property; washing windows that had been recently washed; painting things that hardly needed painting.)

His hair-trigger temper notwithstanding, Ben was not physically abusive. With him it was the persistent threat that something bad could break out at any moment. For a time he had a disciplinary rubber hose, about as long as a forearm, that was really more a metaphorical threat than a punitive one. He deployed it only once, on my butt. My friend and I threw it in the lake. It floated back next to our dock. We buried it. Our dog, Josephine, retrieved it. So we carried it half a mile down the road and placed it in someone's mailbox.

Notwithstanding Ben's intermittent harassments, Diane and I passed a relatively happy and healthy childhood. There were canoe trips and swimming in summer, ice hockey and sledding in winter. We built log cabin jails in the woods and incarcerated playmates, netted frogs on the lily pads, and swung from ropes into the water Tarzan-style.

When I was about twelve, Ben pulled a fast one on me and Diane. One day he informed us that henceforth our surname would be Butkus. I presume that was with my mother's grudging acquiescence. He explained it was because he wanted to adopt us (he never did). Not only did I find the Eastern European appellation clunky, but also I would have to tell all of my friends and teachers to affix a new sticker on my forehead. What was this, Ellis Island? Not least, I felt it was an affront to my real father.

Neither Ben nor my mother was religious, although in her teens Dorothy converted to the Baptist faith because she "liked the music."

We were enrolled at St. Joseph's Elementary School, in nearby Newton, because they believed it offered a superior education and that the nuns would keep us in line. That was a time when sisters held sway in parochial education, and to a third grader the dourly attired "penguins" cut a forbidding presence. The student body fell into two camps, those who believed the sisters concealed bald heads under their starched habits, and those who maintained they were really men. A couple of them actually liked children. In what might have been an early example of a conspiracy theory, there were rumors about the sisters meting out medieval punishments in the boiler room.

I moved on to Newton High School, which occupies a long, flat, single story building that is a drab exemplar of function-over-form 1950s architecture. NHS was still very much a rural outpost, with one wing devoted to technical and agricultural studies. Alighting in public high school following eight years of Catholic captivity was like transferring from Sing Sing to Disneyland: No uniforms, no daily mass, no fake confessions, no catechism, no religion classes, and no bagged lunches. Delicious freedom. The largest part of the graduating student body found work at local enterprises and settled within twenty miles of town. A small group of us, maybe thirty students, was designated as "college prep."

It was a pleasant, undemanding four years. My girlfriend, Pat, and I were voted "Most Likely to Succeed," although she was way more likely than I. More prescient for me would have been "*most-likely-to-succeed-only-to-have-his-face-ripped-off-by-depression-and-left-for-dead-on-the-side-of-the-road.*"

As a measure of NHS's isolation and insularity, the word college did not seriously enter my vocabulary until early junior year with the arrival of the daunting SATs, which I completed with respectable scores.

Aside from serving as editor of the school newspaper, *The Sentinel*, I achieved some extra-curricular renown as the second worst lacrosse player in school history (the lacrosse program had started the year before). While my grades were solid, not stellar, neither Ben nor my mother could offer assistance in the college search, and again, I felt cheated by not having my real father around for guidance.

Ben and my mother entertained frequently. The high point of the evening, at least for me, came when Grandma Dot performed a laudable performance of the Charleston in front of the fireplace. And Ben was a marvelous vocalist, a professional level tenor (in my opinion) in the order of his idol, Mario Lanza. Even when I hated Ben, which was a lot, his singing was something to admire. That usually commenced after about eight gin and tonics, followed by post performance snifters of syrupy Sambuca.

On summer vacations when my friends were swimming and playing ball, I was consigned to Ben's grubby trucking company, a fleet of about twenty massive eighteen-wheelers, where I toiled fourteen hours a day (4:00 p.m. to 6:00 a.m.), six days a week, no pay. (The trucks were on the road all day so maintenance was performed at night). It had to be the grimiest job in Sussex County. I spent most of my groggy time in the grease pit, a narrow trench under the trucks for changing oil, greasing moving parts, and getting filthy. Oleaginous black lubricants penetrated the skin like tattoos and worked their way under the fingernails, taking the entire off season to remove. To clean my hands during the night I had to plunge them into a bin of diesel fuel—try that with a paper cut. Fortunately, I had a girlfriend whose ardent feelings for me superseded the fragrance of petroleum products. I would rather have worked on a chain gang.

Ben maintained that servitude in the garage would expose me to "the other side of life'" and motivate me to do well in school and make something of myself. I countered that a couple of nights observing from the comfort of the air conditioned office could have yielded the same edifying effect. Naturally, I thought about how summers would have passed with my real father, and what kind of something I would have become.

Though the garage was arduous, it had its lighter moments. My favorite character was a bear of a man with a horseradish voice, cleft lip, and scant denture named Al Hughes. He was said to have been a war hero but he never talked about it. Among his estimable skills was drinking an entire quart of milk in one swig. Irrepressibly cheerful and garrulous, on our first night working together, he treated me to play-by-play commentary of his sexual exploits with his wife the night before—followed by a loud roar. The other side of life indeed.

On our first night of working together, Al decreed that my name was Billy and kept it up all summer. He liked to sing pop songs although he rarely knew more than the first line.

One night Al developed a toothache and howled in pain. When it worsened, he grabbed a pair of plyers and dipped them into the diesel fuel.

"Ahhhhhh!" he howled, tossing aside a bloody molar.

I was stunned, and asked if there was anything I could do.

"I don't know, it still hurts."

"Give it a little time; I'll look around for aspirin."

When I was in the office, I heard another loud eruption.

"I pulled the wrong tooth!" he bellowed.

He quickly remedied the situation, and we laughed like hell.

Every so often I was liberated from the grease pit for a leisurely ride in one of the trucks as it made its rounds. Upon reaching a destination I had to unload, by hand, fifty pound bags of powdered lime—in the mid-summer heat. What really disturbed me about all of it was not the summer-wasting-brain-numbing-back-breaking work. It was that Ben never once expressed gratitude. I could tell that he was appreciative in a way, but he could not shed his tough guy persona to express it. On the rare occasions that Ben let down his guard with a guarded compliment or a word of encouragement, I absolutely melted and thought he was the best.

I toiled at the garage in the summers of freshman and sophomore year. The idea of another stint in the grease pit was abhorrent. So I investigated alternatives, mostly of an educational nature that Ben could not veto. Six months prior, I had applied to a summer school for high school journalists. As the next editor of *The Sentinel*, it made sense.

About twenty-five juniors and seniors from around the country were invited on the basis of writing samples. I was accepted.

The Blair Summer School for Journalism, which happened to be only fifteen miles from Newton, was rigorous, and fellow students were bright and ambitious, several notches above the Newton High School college prep group. Under the demanding Blair faculty, my writing improved considerably. We attended classes in the morning and for the rest of the day reported stories in the rural hamlet of Blairstown, which had about eleven inhabitants, or appeared to. When one of the over-interviewed locals saw a student journalist approaching, he or she would hop in a vehicle and peel out over the hill. Blair reinforced my desire to be a journalist. I had to find a college first.

In fairness, Ben was capable of quiet kindness and generosity. When Diane and I were in elementary school, our best friends were Patty and Allen "Thumper" Mulligan. We were inseparable. Their father, also Allen, worked at the Newton Trust Company, a major bank in the county; that is, until he was caught elbow deep in the cash safe. He was charged with embezzling, and there was talk of jail time. Ben did not want our playmates' father going to the big house, so he fronted the money to keep him free and also helped square things with the bank. What is more, he gave Mulligan a bookkeeping job at his trucking company. A year later, my mother, who was helping out with accounting chores in the office, discovered that Mulligan was embezzling *there*, too. Again, Ben covered his bail and arranged for a payback schedule. The family moved after that, and we never saw Patty and Thumper again.

As I grew older, after college, Ben began treating me with respect, even a modicum of warmth. I sometimes imagined what it would have been like if Skippy were to meet Ben. Would they have *anything* in common? I like to think so, but it is doubtful. It would be like two gardeners looking at a tomato plant, each with fixed ideas about how to make it grow. That I made it to an Ivy League university under the blue collar, laissez faire direction of Ben raises the question of how high I would have flourished with my real father.

While my mother rarely brought up Skippy, it was not because she had put those days entirely behind her. Ben sensed that, and I suspect harbored some jealousy regarding his venerated parental predecessor. In 1959, as we were leaving the Bronx and moving into the Lake Lenape house, my mother unpacked a heavy metal movie projector and small screen that stood on a little tripod. They looked like something from Thomas Edison's workshop. We threaded the machine and flicked it on. I was rapt: on the screen, in fairly good quality black-and-white, were Skippy and Dorothy, at an ocean beach. With the scrawny physique of a teenager still in a growth spurt, Skippy mugged for the camera while inflating a beach ball. My mother, trim and playful, was walking from the water toward the camera. What a shock. Here was my father, who barely existed in the hazy past tense, alive and well. For me it was more powerful than could be imagined, a cascade of emotions—amazement, elation, love, and grief. My mother sat quietly on the couch. Ben was stoic. Following the show no one said a word. Ben unspooled the film, returned the projector to its carrying case, and placed it in a laundry closet outside of my bedroom, covered with blankets. From time to time I would uncover it and think about the magic it possessed. One day I lifted the blankets and it was not there.

"Where's the movie projector?" I asked my mother.

"I don't know," she replied, unconvincingly.

I searched the house. My guess is that Ben disposed of it.

A little over a year later, before Christmas, I was doing my homework on the kitchen table, and my mother was washing the dinner dishes. Without turning around, she asked, "Do you know what today is?"

"Nope."

"It's December 10. This is the day your father died."

I should have felt sad, but my mother had caught me off guard. I did not know what to say. I said nothing; nor did she, which was strange, like saying "I wrecked the car" and leaving it at that.

The following year again I was doing my homework at the kitchen table, and she was cooking.

"Do you know what today is?"

"The day my father died?"

"Yes."

I supposed this called for some inquiry on my part. What was it like to die of lupus?

I was eager for more, but, again, I could not think of suitable questions. The third year came around—I was older, bolder, and more prepared. My homework was spread out on the kitchen table—by that time I had my own room and a desk, but I was not going to miss it.

She said nothing.

I sat patiently.

She began making sandwiches for our school lunch. (As a time saver, she would make six or eight tuna salad sandwiches and freeze them; at school, when they thawed, I ate them with a spoon.)

After ten minutes, I moved to the living room to see what was on TV.

My mother came in and sat on the couch, reading the *Newark Evening News*. I attempted to stir up a little general conversation.

"Mom, I bet I could train Josephine [our dog] to fetch the newspaper and bring it into the kitchen."

"Do you know what day it is?" she asked.

"Yes, I do," I replied.

By that time I was mature enough to sense it was as much about her as it was about me. I wanted to know what she was feeling at the time. Was that her catharsis, seven words? I have come to believe that she wanted the memory of my father to glimmer like a Christmas ornament, if only for one day a year, after she was gone. She never mentioned December 10 again, nor did she need to.

As I finished high school, Ben no doubt believed that his school of hard knocks had paid off—good grades, decent SAT scores, newspaper editor, no drugs or booze. Of course he would not pin a medal on my chest or anything like that. One evening at dinnertime, a family friend, Ralph Roberts—a barrel-chested, hilarious man who was one of my favorite adults—dropped by the house. Ralphie (aka Rotten Ralphie) was in the tombstone trade and always joked that my rock was in his warehouse waiting for an inscription. I was in the other room playing with Josephine.

"What is Bryan doing these days?" he asked Ben.

"He's going to Columbia this fall—journalism," replied Ben with uncharacteristic pride.

I believe it was the first time he had ever mentioned the school. None of his other children had finished college, and I am sure it was a disappointment.

CHAPTER 11
Deadline

MY UNDERGRADUATE YEARS WERE PASSED at Colgate University, in the tundra of New York State, where twice we frolicked in minor snowstorms on my birthday, May 17. A beautiful school with stone buildings dating to 1819, Colgate did not offer journalism classes. Impressively, though, the school of barely two thousand scholars supported two student newspapers. I did not contribute, largely because I was so stressed out trying to keep up in an academic environment worlds away from agrarian Newton High School.

My first reality check came when I met my roommate Jon, who was from a nationally ranked high school outside of Washington, DC. His parents were doctors, and he planned to be a doctor. He brought along many, many books on all subjects, including novels, and read at least one or two a week aside from his pre-med requirements. The first week he gifted me a tome on ornithology. I arrived at college with a paperback dictionary.

My major in school was changing to an easier major. Ultimately I contrived a scholastic farrago called American Studies, and persuaded a skeptical professor to sign off on it. (Today American Studies is a more widely recognized field of scholarship, thanks to me.) In late junior year I applied to half a dozen journalism graduate programs around the country. The first response arrived in a very official looking letter from the Columbia University Graduate School of Journalism.

The school admitted roughly one out of every hundred applicants, so I had considered it more or less a waste of a stamp. In what may have been a colossal clerical error, I was accepted.

Having grown up in the country and attended college in an even more rural environs, arriving at Columbia was a shock. The school's main campus is on 116th Street and Broadway, bordering Harlem and near two menacing parks. In 1975, the mismanaged city was on its knees, down to pocket change, and had to be taken over by a state agency. Manhattan was filthy, dangerous, and inefficient. The graffiti-marred subway doubled as a hoodlums' clubhouse. Arriving students at the J-School were handed a map of the greater university neighborhood that, rather than point out cultural amenities and restaurants, identified places *not to go*.

The journalism program was demanding and hectic. Unlike other such schools where the curriculum included courses like public relations and media studies, Columbia was strictly about reporting and writing. Every morning I found in my mailbox a daily assignment. It could be to cover a labor strike at Kennedy airport, attend a political function, spend the day at City Hall, or cover happenings on Wall Street. The assignments were to be turned in at the end of the day for faculty comments. The next day we started all over again.

I volunteered to cover the New York Stock Exchange because my father's best friend—and the person who, with his brother, Ed, provided me with a real Christmas days after my father's death—would be available for an interview. Al Franklin, a gentle, soft-spoken patrician from Westchester, treated me to lunch in the historic Bull and Bear Club, a cool, dark private bar and restaurant aromatic of old money and fine cigars. We talked about our families, my plans after school, and my Columbia assignment. Then, without prompting, he reminisced:

"You know, I think of your father every day," he said, his eyes glistening over. "Shortly before he passed he said, 'Please keep an eye on Bryan. He is going to have a hard time with this.'"

I think Al had wanted to say that for a long time. He had, indeed, checked in with me from time to time. We remained in sporadic communication over the years and our families were close, but I did not exactly feel watched over.

Upon graduation, the country was in a serious recession, and journalism jobs were scarce. A Columbia faculty member tipped me off to a position at the *Journal Inquirer,* a pugnacious little daily northeast of Hartford, Connecticut. It turned out to be an ideal place to start a career.

One of the most important assets a rookie reporter can have is capable editors to mentor you in writing, reporting, story execution, ethics, and so on. (And it's healthy to get hollered at once in a while, too.) The *Journal Inquirer* was a great place to learn. It covered about ten medium to small towns northeast of Hartford. Being the new guy, I was dispatched to cover the smallest of all, Suffield, a mere pebble on the New England map that was best known for (only known for) a reputable prep school called Suffield Academy.

The *JI* was an afternoon paper, which meant my deadline was 10:00 a.m. It was my panicked responsibility to fill the Suffield page, three stories a day. Suffield does not even have a downtown. There were about seven thousand courteous New Englanders in residence, and disappointingly little crime. I may have accosted every single adult in town—at the grocery store, church, the post office—pleading for story ideas. Somehow I filled those pages for nearly two years.

CHAPTER 12
Women

FOR REASONS DESCRIBED IN A previous chapter, I arrived at my peak dating stage as ripe for disaster as the Hindenburg. It would be nearly a decade before I gained any insight into the pathology driving it all. My unwitting love-hate relationships with women—"hate" is overstating it—reached full bloom as my professional life commenced.

One of my first post-college romantic adventures occurred when I was at the *JI*. I had been invited to a Christmas party at the *Hartford Courant*—I do not know why, as I knew no one at the paper. They must have been impressed by my incisive reporting on the Suffield sewer board. My eyes fell upon a tall, slender, chestnut-haired woman who turned out to be an editor at the paper. Being too shy to insinuate myself into her circle of conversation, I stood sentry at the bar—it was a newspaper party, after all, where *everyone* visits the bar. Soon she arrived in the company of two male reporters.

"Don't you work at the *JI*?" one of them asked me.

"Yes, I do," I replied.

"Go for it, man," he said, extending his hand.

The *JI* was barely a fourth the size of the *Courant*, but was greatly respected in news circles for its kick ass, take-no-prisoners approach to regional reporting.

We circulated with drinks and hors d'oeuvres until the guys peeled away. Jessica was two years older than I. She was on the serious side,

typical for a news editor, so I had to flip through my notepad of levity
to get a rise out of her. Having grown up in Lafayette, Louisiana, she
was a knowledgeable Cajun cook. That was before chef Paul Prud-
homme came blazing onto the scene, so it was quite exotic. We hit
it off, having many similar interests, particularly food. Predictably, I
became very smitten very quickly—way too quickly. Looking back, I
see that it was not a normal, healthy smitten, but rather a needy and a
vulnerable one, which was to become a destructive template. We dated
and passed enjoyable days off exploring the area.

For my birthday she prepared two classic Cajun dishes, and when
I arrived at her house it smelled like a spice factory. She had been
cooking for hours. Jessica scooped some rice onto my dish and then
added a couple of pieces of poultry smothered in a thick, energetically
seasoned sauce.

"Mange bien!" she beamed.

"Wow, looks great. What is it called?"

"*Lapin Sauce Piquant* ... Rabbit in Spicy Cajun Sauce!"

"Lapin?"

"Enjoy, honey!"

Now you have to understand: it was 1975. Regular humans did
not eat bunnies at that point, at least not American humans. The
French had been enjoying them for centuries; then again, they also
like poached calf's brain. It would not be until the 1990s that rabbit
became widespread on American menus, by which time I was reviewing bunny dishes without making a fuss.

I excused myself to "wash my hands" and snatched some paper
towels from the kitchen. I tasted the sauce, which was extraordinary, a
fusillade of dried peppers and spices, so precisely calibrated that they
ignited sequentially over the tongue.

"I forgot the bread!" Jessica exclaimed as she headed toward the
kitchen. I quickly transferred a sizeable quantity of the meat into the
paper towels and rested them on my lap, where they immediately
leaked onto my blue pants. When Jessica departed again, to get a

bottle of red wine, I transferred the sodden package to my sports jacket perched on the back of my chair. When I raved about the rabbit she happily informed me that she was on familiar terms with a butcher who had access to "fresh killed," so we could have it whenever we wanted.

We dated for nine happy months—or at least I was happy—before, abruptly, she accepted a big position at the *Atlanta Journal-Constitution*. "I hate New England winters," she declared almost matter of factly.

It was all sweet and apologetic, but she did not even ask if I would consider going with her. It was as if people did that all the time— abruptly fracture relationships in order to relocate to another state, citing meteorological benefits. Being in the same peripatetic profession I should have been prepared for this.

Still, it was quite a blow. A normal jettisoned beau would feel down in the dumps for a week or two. But this threw me into a tailspin that I had never experienced, wildly inappropriate to the circumstances. Headaches, nausea, insomnia, loss of appetite. I drove four hours to upstate New York to be with a friend. The acute symptoms subsided in about a month, but the anxiety persisted far longer.

The plot was more or less the same with damsel number two, only in reverse. Tall, lithesome, athletic (and rich), Trish was a Meryl Streep type, and very much into the equine set. That is how I met her, covering a polo match, about which I knew virtually nothing. She was an architect. Her family owned half a dozen shiny horses that were bred for competitions. On our second date—"Let's go riding!"—I flounced atop a trotting beast for less than a minute before taking flight and landing on a riverbed, breaking my thumb. Fortunately, that was not a deal breaker.

By all measures, she was ideal—kind, fun, thoughtful, and bright. An added allure was that her life was so at variance with mine. We travelled throughout New England. We went to Ireland. She even met my parents. After about eight months, though, I felt myself pulling away, for no discernible reason. It was like wanting to leave a well-pay- ing, career-track job because ... well, I will probably get fired at some point, so let's avoid the humiliation. Although in my case it would be angst and incipient depression. I continued to experience a disquiet bordering on fear. Might she leave me? Should I gallop out of town on the next stallion? I tried to banish those thoughts but as the weeks passed, my disengagement grew. In what became my signature stratagem, I did not definitively "break-up," as mature, mentally sound people do; rather I watched it slowly unravel, like the head bandages on Claude Rains in *The Invisible Man*. Then I was gone. And another painful crash. Astoundingly, I was clueless.

My preternatural fear of separation, it turned out, was not entirely gender specific. While working at the *JI*, I resided in a two-family New England style house with wide porches, tall windows, and Gothic filigree in the moribund former mill town of Rockville. (It is proudly known as the childhood home of the hugely popular 1960s singer Gene Pitney—*Town without Pity, The Man Who Shot Liberty Valance*.) Across the hall lived a couple from Maine, Phil and Janet Crossman. He was a carpenter, a house painter, and a fine humor writer. She worked at an insurance company in Hartford. We became very close, and they joked that they were the parents of a hapless teenager, which was not far from the truth. We had another, older, friend, Wendell Stevenson, who also looked out for me. I fondly recall Saturday mornings when we convened what was called the Misty Crow Breakfast Club (Miller Stevenson Crossman), with a breathtaking quantity of New England victuals.

One day Phil informed me that he and Janet had decided to return to Vinalhaven, Maine, an island in Penobscot Bay where Phil's extended family had lived for generations. My initial reaction was anger. Then alarm. Over the following days, I persuaded myself that it was no big deal. I could visit them frequently. It was *only* a six hour drive to the ferry in good weather.

On the day of their departure I found myself in Montpelier, Vermont, more than three hours away. Why Montpelier? I wasn't sure; all I knew was that I could not be at the house when they drove off, no way. After a little tourism and a beer-drenched lunch, I drove around the countryside killing time. My heart was racing thinking of the moving van. I felt terrible not saying goodbye. What message would that send? But I could not do it—I could not stand there and watch them trundle out of my life. I would lose it. Phil and Janet remained on the Island. I visited them every summer. It was ten years before I brought up my disappearance with Phil. He said that he had been wondering about it all that time.

I returned to Rockville at 6:00 p.m. On the lawn were an old caneback chair and a small round table with a broken leg. I climbed the stairs and entered their living room where the couch and the television used to be, and where we watched movies and hung out. The setting sun filtered through the pine trees, casting golden shards of light over the dark green walls. The familiar sensation of anxiety and profound loss welled up inside me. I lay on the floor, facing the ceiling, holding my head, and sobbed for I don't know how long.

As troublesome and puzzling as my female separations were, I attempted to write them off as aberrations, something all red-blooded young men experience while scaling the bluffs of young romance. Still, my behavior could be cruel, in a passive aggressive way. I began to consider that there might something driving it, but what?

College students in Psychology 101 are introduced to the concept of cognitive dissonance, a term widely misused to mean "confused" or "ambivalent." It is closer to rationalizing. For example, I may consider myself a kind and moral individual. However, I may do something demonstratively unkind, maybe cruel, like ungraciously breaking off a relationship. The mind does not abide contradictions, and will seek ways to set things right. In that scenario, the blame is shifted so that the other person brought on the breakup and "deserved it." That is as convenient as it can be malicious.

After two years at the *JI*, I deemed myself ready for the big time. I applied to a number of larger newspapers and other publications, including the Associated Press, the world's largest news gathering organization. The way it works at the AP is, if you pass the tests, you are placed on a waiting list. Subsequently, you are assigned to the first bureau that has an opening. It could be Boston or Chicago or Sacramento or Miami or even a dull backwater like Oklahoma City. I was sent to Oklahoma City. After all, it *was* the AP, and it could be fun living someplace so different from my home.

My office was in the drab basement of the *Daily Oklahoman*, the state's major newspaper. It was like a bomb shelter from the 1950s minus the canned goods. On the wall was a giant red bell that sounded *only* for hair-on-fire events: tornadoes, assassinations, UFO landings, or the death of a celebrity like the Pope or Elvis Presley. On a steamy night in August 1977, Elvis the Pelvis hip-swiveled off of his mortal stage. He did so on a slow news night, and on my shift, which was considerate of him. I was allowed to report and write several breathless tributes, all with tenuous regional angles—he once stopped for bagels and coffee at Mel's Diner, or maybe it was a corn muffin. No sooner had the stories gone out over the wires than I was designated the Elvis authority of the Southwestern United States. Though not even an Elvis fan, I was recruited for television and radio interviews for days.

My work shift was 4:00 p.m. to midnight, so opportunities for a robust social life were limited. Further curbing the excitement was a peculiar local statute: Oklahoma City had many bars but they could not serve you a drink. Let me explain. Following the repeal of Prohibition, in 1933, the vast majority of states legalized alcohol sales. Not Oklahoma. Upon arriving in 1977, I discovered that you could not walk into an establishment and order a beer or a cocktail. Legally, you had to belong to this or that "social club," the requirement for membership being a desire to have a drink. Membership cards were not difficult to secure—waiters and waitresses were happy to pass them out. It was a total sham; if anything, it sanctioned excessive imbibing.

Even more bizarre, the law stated that you could drink only from your own bottle, with your name on it, that was stowed behind the bar. For example, if you wanted a gin and tonic from your bottle, the bar provided "setup." (Glass, tonic, ice cubes.) Apparently there were state liquor inspectors, but I never saw one. Every couple of years, there was a "liquor by the drink" referendum to end all of the nonsense, and every time the rural conservative Christians shot it down. Finally, in 1984, the bill passed, with 51 percent of the vote.

Shortly after arriving in Oklahoma City I dropped in to a lively place downtown called the VZD Lounge. I dutifully requested a membership card, which was unconditionally provided. There I bumped into an attractive, wine loving vegetarian named Diane. Tall, thin, and with a bright smile and languorous southwestern accent, she was a social magnet for a large group of convivial friends in their mid-twenties. They enthusiastically adopted me.

Diane was an extraordinary vegetarian cook. Before long we were having midnight dinners at her house after my shift—she worked nights as well, at a rental car office. Diane liked *Pouilly-Fuissé*. I had never tasted *Pouilly-Fuissé*, nor any fine wine for that matter. It was a revelation: bright, fruity yet dry, and with a flinty mineral edge. That set me on the road to being a part-time wine writer.

Diane had a hot car, a green Datsun Z, and on our days off we dashed around the state. Oklahoma has an monotonous topography, straw colored and as flat as a crêpe pan with the exception of the verdant and hilly Tulsa area. Diane seemed to be acquainted with or related to half the population of the state. We were always busy. Dining-out options were limited unless you had a hankering for chicken-fried steak (beef cutlets dipped in egg and flour and pan fried) or fried chicken. (Survival tip: Do not order Chinese food in Oklahoma.)

Diane was sweet, smart, and curious and felt intellectually constrained in the Southwest. I began talking about moving back East. She hinted that she, too, would consider moving. That set off my Elvis bell. If she were to follow me when I returned to New Jersey or New York, the reasoning went, something sad would ensue, and she would leave. I would be a cripple once more. In an uncommonly mature and candid moment, I volunteered that I would be going home sooner than later, to an uncertain future, and that I could not make any commitments. Let's take it month by month. Agreed. Diane then added that she would be taking a driving tour of the Northeast within the next several months, and she kindly offered to bring back any belongings that did not fit in my car.

In the fall of 1978, I moved back to Sussex County, taking up residence with a friend, Stuart Ring, a bachelor physician who lived on a small dairy farm ten miles from Newton. His misadventures with women nearly approximated mine in intensity, if not in quantity. He recounted that when he was a medical resident at Manhattan's Bellevue Hospital he lived with his wife nearby. He went off to work one morning, and upon returning, discovered everything gone: furniture, TV, bed, rugs, kitchenware, dental floss, toilet paper. Empty.

"I ate out that night," he said.

I never heard the other side of the story.

On the farm I was looking forward to a placid Jeffersonian country life without drama or social complications—tending the cattle, helping with farm chores, thinking about my future, and doing some freelance writing on the side. The "downtown" of our hamlet, named Hainesburg, was little more than a dozen leprous buildings and a collection of scruffy houses flanking Route 94 near the Delaware Water Gap. Adult recreation was limited to a handful of dim, uninviting bars, one in a turreted, rundown former hotel that looked as if a good breeze could knock it over.

On my second day in town, I drove to the post office. Standing in line I felt a tap on my shoulder. I turned to behold a stunning young Japanese woman in tight jeans, a blue blouse, and pale yellow scarf. She had to be five foot ten, in her early twenties, which made her even more fetching. I forget what her question was. We got to talking, as we were both new to town. That evening we went to the least menacing of the bars, later joined by a curious Stuart.

So much for Jefferson. Overnight, the placid country life turned action-packed and exciting. It was like waterskiing on Walden Pond.

A native of Colorado, Wendy was an all-American cheerleader type, a flight attendant for United Airlines who had recently rented part of a house that was within walking distance of the farm. That was almost more than I could handle. Wendy, always cheerful, always up for new adventures, had lots of time off, which meant I took a lot of time off. We toured the area, cooked lavish dinners, paddled canoes on the Delaware River, and explored the Pocono Mountains. To be honest, we did not have much in common, which gave me pause. But not too much pause.

One glistening fall afternoon, Wendy and I were sunning on the dock of a small pond behind the farmhouse. I heard hollering coming from the porch. Stuart was gesticulating wildly. I walked toward him when I espied, parked near the barn, a green Datsun Z. I don't know if I was more alarmed or ashamed. Again, I had hurt a woman, and with little self awareness. Diane appeared to accept the situation with equanimity. I think we all had dinner that evening.

Summer turned to a punishing winter. Wendy had a huge fireplace, and we had stocked plenty of wine. It was very much a fantasy life. One day I received a call from the *Providence Journal Bulletin*, a reputable New England newspaper, with an offer of employment. Following seven months of pampered living, I needed income. The paper sounded ideal. Once again, my stomach tightened. I became convinced, with no evidence, that if Wendy were to move to Providence with me she would depart before long. And by that point I understood the consequences of such events.

In Providence, I nested in an airy Victorian style home on the city's stately East Side, featuring two grand fireplaces and a small kitchen. On my first week in residence, before I had unpacked the cutlery, a bundle of mail arrived at my door, addressed to one Helen Tomlinson (Second floor). It was a scene out of a Neil Simon farce. I walked upstairs and knocked. The door opened, and I nearly fell over the bannister. The woman's face was plastered with white cream, revealing only her glistening blue eyes. She wore a turban of sorts and a thin cotton bathrobe. I turned over the mail and took flight.

The following evening, Helen, with her flawless Nordic skin on full display, came visiting, carrying a bottle of wine. It occurred to me that this might be a good time to join the Peace Corps in Micronesia. Hadn't I tripped over the wires of youthful passion one too many times? Clearly, something was wrong with me. Then again, some things were very right. I stoked a fire in the hearth. Helen and I enjoyed the wine. She never spent another night in her apartment.

Vivacious and irrepressibly cheerful, with Beatles-style golden bangs and a quick sense of humor, she had just enrolled in graduate school at the prestigious Rhode Island School of Design. Keeping to the familiar script, I became very close very quickly; she could be the one.

We lived several blocks from Brown University, so there was always something going on. In 1978, Providence was a gray and grumpy metropolis, having lost much of its manufacturing base (textiles, furniture) to the more economical southern states. It was once known as the costume jewelry capital of the country, but beginning in the 1970s that industry as well hopped the rails to cheaper venues. The city did not stage its extraordinary comeback until the early 2000s, long after my time. Today it is a handsome, vivacious town with some magnificent seventeenth and eighteenth century architecture and some of the best dining in New England.

The "Ocean State" is the most beautiful place I have ever lived, with the open sea visible nearly at every turn. It was inexpensive, easygoing, and only an hour from Boston. I discovered that there was a reputable culinary program within walking distance of our home, at Johnson & Wales University. I signed up for some basic courses—Classic Sauces, Seafood, and Introduction to Pastries—but given the unpredictability of a newspaper life, my attendance was spotty.

One day a chest freezer in a flannel shirt showed up at the door—Helen's ex-boyfriend. Only he appeared to be unenlightened about the "ex" part. The man with a red beard looked at me as if I weren't worthy of being beaten up. They moved outside to talk for a long time, and drove around the block. After about an hour, Helen came back and sadly announced that she was returning to him.

That was like an ice pick through the eye. It was my worst smash-up ever. For the first two days I remained catatonic on the couch. The following day, I drove north of Boston and holed up with friends. I was so physically ill that they took me to the local emergency room, where I told the doctor I was dying of nothing. For two days my friends proffered whatever therapy they could, and I limped home. Helen was waiting in front of the fireplace with a big smile. It was like switching on the light. I was fine, but not really fine.

Several months later we decided that it made little sense to pay for an unoccupied apartment. We moved into a cottage on magnificent Narragansett Bay, where the tidal sea was so clean we plucked qua-hogs (Rhode Island's term for large clams) from the waters off of our beach to make chowder. We hosted dinners and barbecues and sailed to Block Island. It was ideal.

Like all good things in my life, it was destined to end—or more precisely, I was destined to end it, without an awareness of why. At that point, I was contacted about an editor's job at *Connecticut Magazine*, in Fairfield, Connecticut, where I had freelanced in the past. While my life at the *Journal* was content enough, there appeared little opportunity for meaningful advancement. That was partly a matter of geography. Rhode Island is thirty-seven miles wide and forty-eight miles long, less than half the size of Delaware. A local quip goes that Rhode Islanders consider a drive of more than fifteen minutes a road trip. The *Journal*, at the time, was a prosperous company with a large news staff. *Journal* reporters were everywhere, behind every tree, outside of schools, atop every sand dune. There was not much room to stretch, or advance.

The position at *Connecticut Magazine*—it was a serious news publica-tion at the time—was enticing: senior editor. My interview with the boss went well, so well in fact, that, amplifying my culinary school credentials, I tossed out the idea of writing some restaurant reviews. She said yes. It was a less demanding age.

When I decided to accept the job, Helen and I discussed what to do. You don't need to be Dr. Phil to foretell what came next. Helen was six months from graduation, and she had begun seeking employment as an industrial designer. Again, the tornado bell. She would leave me, sooner or later. Maybe the lumbering Frigidaire would return. Typically, I waffled and muttered noncommittal gibberish about our future. For eighteen hours we were unofficially engaged. It all came down to a non-decision, my favored approach to issues of the amorous nature.

Did I love Helen? I believe I did. Was the feeling mutual? Yes. Did we get along? Yes. Were there undisclosed issues that could arise, like massive debt or a gambling addiction? Not likely. As with Wendy, I kicked the can down the road hoping things would resolve themselves. Nothing resolves itself. Being fearful to make decisions is a common trait of depression, as I would soon understand.

I moved into a miniscule apartment on the loft level of a barn in coastal Fairfield, Connecticut—not a charming renovated barn but rather a battered old wreck that retained heat like a screen door. On blustery nights it swayed like a tacking sailboat. Why I moved there I cannot say. Helen and I burned a lot of gas driving back and forth, and it was taking a toll on our relationship. It appeared that Helen was to receive a job offer in San Francisco. I *encouraged* her to accept it, adding, disingenuously, that I would give some thought as to what to do. Then I met Anne.

CHAPTER 13
France

1983

Anne and I had been together for nearly four eventful years, and for the first time we had achieved the status of employed citizens—I had started at the *Times* and she was busy with freelance work. We had never seriously discussed marriage, and certainly not in the past year-and-a-half when, for me, the act of getting dressed was considered a praise-worthy triumph. We agreed that it was time to make it official and escape on vacation, to France. Our wedding was a relatively small affair, held on our lawn overlooking Long Island Sound on a glorious spring afternoon. Anne wore a white dress with wild flowers in her hair. About a dozen *Times* colleagues were in attendance. Our friends from Restaurant du Village, Charley and Priscilla, made a magnificent three-tier wedding cake. A country music band set up in the garage.

Our first French destination was Soustres, Anne's family compound. It was my second visit, the first "en famille." I was treated warmly, especially as I had made much progress with Anne's French lessons. It was to be a quick stopover, with plans to dine at one of the most revered restaurants in France, La Pyramid, in the village of Vienne, a few hours' drive east. On our first day Anne introduced me to local markets that her family had frequented for decades where I was introduced to luscious, sweet tomatoes, crisp purple artichokes, pencil thin wild asparagus, apricots and figs, oysters, Mediterranean seafood, game, cèpes, and chanterelles. I remember sampling the regional dish *bourride*, a fabulous monkfish and vegetable stew thickened with heady aioli (a rich garlic mayonnaise) and traditional little seafood pies called *tielles*.

La Pyramid was the creation of the late owner and chef Fernand Point, who is celebrated as the father of modern French cuisine. Abjuring the complex and often heavy fare that had characterized French gastronomy for more than a century, he lightened dishes and pioneered many new cooking techniques that set the stage for nouvelle cuisine in the 1970s. Among his well-known pupils were Paul Bocuse (L'Auberge du Pont de Collonges, Lyon), Alain Chapel (Restaurant Alain Chapel, in Mionnay), and Pierre and Jean Troisgros (Troisgros, Ouches).

Point was a roomy and opinionated man whose midday meal was accompanied by a bottle of champagne. One of his oft-quoted gastronomic maxims was: "When I go to a restaurant I always shake the hand of the chef. If he is thin, I will probably dine poorly. If he is both thin and sad, the only hope is in flight."

I had looked forward to that visit for years. Point died in 1955; his wife, Marie-Louise, ran the establishment until late in life. It closed in 1986. The night before our celebratory meal, I felt my barometer plunging. "No. No. No!" That cannot be happening, not before our excitedly anticipated meal. By the time we pulled into the village of Vienne, identified by a large stone obelisk in the center of town, I was in a trancelike depressed state, fearful of passing through the door entering the dining room.

We entered the exquisite white dining room and passed a cadre of cherubic waiters who looked too young to have a driver's license. My brain felt as if it was muted with cotton balls; a stress headache came on for good measure. My desire was to hold myself together enough not to spoil Anne's experience. We ordered a white Burgundy, Chassagne-Montrachet, one of my favorites. It was typically silken and sumptuous, but on that day it failed to summon the angels. It was just good wine to tamp down the surging anxiety. I wanted to run out the door, taking down a couple of the altar boys on the way. It was horrific.

The food was surprisingly simple, and perfect.

Cavaillon melon

Salade of ecrivisse (crayfish) in a light herbal broth with truffles

Rack of lamb with tarragon sauce

Turbot with champagne sauce and mushrooms

Bavaroise des apricot (a rich, egg-based custard thickened with cream, with apricots and a coulis of raspberries)

Tragically, I could not flee, and to where? We passed a few more difficult days at Soustres, and returned to Westport to an uncertain fate.

Chapter 14
Pierre

ONE AFTERNOON WHEN I WAS visiting the *Times'* office—I was a free-lancer at the time—editor Ward introduced me to a genial silver haired man named Pierre Franey. I recognized him from his cook-book covers, and for years had followed his recipe column called the 60-Minute Gourmet, which he produced with longtime collaborator Craig Claiborne. The two also wrote a weekly column in the paper's Sunday magazine as well as feature stories and books.

Pierre possessed an infectious joie de vie that made him enjoyable to be around. He was raised in a small village in Burgundy, steeped in a rich food culture going back centuries. It was not uncommon that he donned a cook's apron when he was only fourteen years old. With the encouragement of a family friend, he made his way to Paris for an exhausting and sometimes brutal life of a novice cook in classic restau-rants. Within four years he found himself at one of Paris's most august establishments, named Drouant. Despite his considerable experience, he was hired as a lowly *commis*, a position a notch above water boy on a football squad. That is not to say he was disrespected. It was just the way things worked.

That was 1939, and the drums of war were intensifying throughout Europe. It also happened to be the first of two summers of the New York World's Fair. Up until the 1960s, World's Fairs were occasions of pride and excitement, with each participating nation trying to outdo the others showing off advances in science, architecture, sundry inventions and, of course, food. These global showcases drew hundreds of thousands of visitors. The French government endeavored to show off the best of its country's culinary heritage at a sprawling restaurant called Le Pavillon. Recruited to staff the restaurant were some of the brightest stars in France's gastronomic firmament. Pierre was offered a post as fish cook, quite a recognition of his young talents. Le Pavillon was an overwhelming success, and introduced thousands of Americans to haute French cuisine while sowing the seeds of a French dining renaissance in New York City that persisted into the 1980s.

The opening night menu of Le Pavillon was straightforward and light by the standards of classic French cuisine. Then again, the kitchen prepared more than a thousand dinners daily (136,261 over the summer season), so much had to be setup in advance.

By the time the second summer season of the fair wound to a close, France was gasping under the heel of German occupation. Rather than return to an uncertain fate in France, Pierre remained in New York to plan his next move. Ultimately he enlisted in the American military in hopes of liberating his native land.

At the time of his voluntary induction into the United States Army, Pierre was insistent that he be dispatched to fight in France. However the wartime military, he learned, was not like a restaurant, where you could pick and choose. Besides, the government had another assignment in mind. Pierre was summoned to the Pentagon, where a French-speaking officer lauded his background as a chef and added that there was a prestigious position available, and he would be a perfect fit: personal cook for a General Douglas MacArthur, in the Pacific.

Pierre replied that he did not want to go to the Pacific, he wanted to fight in France—and he had never heard of this General MacArthur. Pierre was held up in Washington, DC for two days as they endeavored to crack his Gallic impertinence.

"I knew my rights," Pierre told me. "As a non-citizen I could not be transferred to war zones against my will."

Exasperated by his insolence, the officer remitted him to the Army's rudimentary cooks' and bakers' school, in Alabama—an assignment inferior even to the one in his teenage days as a *commis*. In the end, however, Pierre got his wish: in the war's receding months his division liberated his Burgundian village.

Again a civilian, Pierre was hired at the Manhattan incarnation of Le Pavillon, on East 55th Street, ultimately rising to the position of executive chef. Some years later, Craig Claiborne, the *Times*' food editor, hailed Pierre as "the greatest chef in America."

Naturally, I was thrilled to make Pierre's acquaintance. Later that day, Ward beckoned me to his desk and divulged that Pierre and Craig had experienced a "falling out." Would I like to be his new professional partner? (The falling out stemmed from Pierre spending so much time working with Craig, who lived nearby in East Hampton, Long Island, that he had little time to devote to his family. His wife, Betty, put her foot down. Pierre put his foot down with Craig. It didn't end well.)

While Pierre was the exalted chef, he was not a writer, at least not in English, thus the collaboration. For more than a dozen years, we worked together on columns, feature stories, books, travel articles, and television programs; he became my most valued friend and a second father. Of course, I could not have had a better restaurant reviewing partner.

I have never seen a man more content and comfortable with his lot in life. Preparing food that gave pleasure to others was his single-minded passion. I passed many happy days at his home in Amagansett, Long Island, with Betty and their son Jacques—and some nearly suicidal ones as well. Like a shifty riverboat gambler, depression does not play fair. I so looked forward to working with Pierre at the beach house. In summer we cooked for two or three days wearing shorts and T-shirts. In the evening we had a tasting dinner with fine wine. I should have paid the *Times* for it. On too many occasions the good times were sucked dry by the beast. I turned silent and took many naps, while Pierre, presumably unaware of my infirmity, carried on alone.

In 1993, a friend at the publishing house Alfred A. Knopf expressed interest in a book about Pierre's extraordinary life. It would be a team project along with Rick Flaste, a longtime editor at the *Times*, and would be written in Pierre's jaunty style.

I was in horrible shape for most of the undertaking, with difficulty reading no less writing. The extreme and erratic cycling left me like a barnacle on a plunging whale.

Rick did a masterful job with the text—the portrait was warm, historical, funny, ironic, and inspirational. I largely devoted myself to organizing the recipes. I was so embarrassed to let Rick down on the project, and fail to do right by Pierre, that when the book was published I could not read it. *A Chef's Tale* has resided on my bookshelf, unopened, for more than twenty-five years. I retrieved it the other day to fact check for this book and then hastily returned it to its longtime home. Merely looking at the cover transports me back to that terrible time.

Eventually my affliction took a toll on my relationship with Pierre. I never confided in him about my problems but he must have picked up on my elastic moods. There were times when, aside from work, I all but ignored him (and everybody else). I think it was hurtful. Sadly, we drifted apart as my comportment became more mercurial and self-involved. He found new writing partners and carried on, although we remained friends.

One October morning in 1996 I received a call from André Soltner, chef and owner of the legendary Lutèce restaurant, in Midtown Manhattan. Pierre had passed away. Fittingly, I suppose, he was on a cruise ship conducting a cooking class. At the conclusion, he repaired to his stateroom to nap. He never awoke. As with so many people who crossed my path in those dark days, I have so many unasked questions and apologies.

Chapter 15
The Reluctant Critic

NEARLY A YEAR LATER, ANNE and I embarked on a vacation to Italy, a risky idea considering the intensifying illness, but she felt a change of scenery might perk me up. Much of my first year as a *Times* staff member entailed a series of waterboardings paired with periods of lucidity and great productivity. There was a fair chance that on that vacation the floor would fall in, but I resolved to give it the old Venetian try. On the flight over, I was nervous and largely silent, pretending to read while availing myself of numerous thumb-sized bottles of vodka.

Anne's plan was to keep my wheels spinning with little down time for glum self-reflection. In Venice, we took residence in the Hotel Danieli, as close as you can get to heaven without divine intervention. The hotel is in a fourteenth-century Venetian palace that overlooks a busy waterway called St. Mark's Basin. One could spend a morning admiring the ornate Byzantine architecture with its aged pink façade, white turrets, marble sills, and romantic balconies with pointed arches.

The general manager, whom I had encountered in New York, was aware of our visit so we were never far from a solicitous staff member. For one of the few times in my life I was not on a working vacation, that is, on assignment for one publication or another. In our first few days, my mood was tentatively upbeat, and we dined at some wonderful trattorias recommended by my friend Danny Meyer, the owner of Union Square Cafe, in Manhattan. In the cafe's dining room transpired one of the more humorous episodes of my reviewing career, something that Danny and I have retold dozens of times.

Union Square Cafe opened in 1985; I became the *Times* restaurant critic just months before, in 1984. We had been friends for more than two years; in fact, I had accompanied him when he was scouting possible locations for his restaurant.

When the Union Square Cafe opened its doors, I faced a blatant journalistic conflict of interest: If I were too soft on Danny's place and gave it an unwarranted stellar review, I would rightly be called out for it. On the other hand, in the unlikely event the restaurant turned out to be a dud, I was not going to poleaxe a friend. A negative *Times* review of a newly opened establishment could well shut it down. So I decided—without informing Danny—that if there were major shortcomings I would not write it up at all. Moreover, during my visits I would pretend to be a stranger to Danny, and him to me.

I arrived with Anne at the handsome clubby bar where customers were avidly slurping oysters. The low-ceilinged dining room was casual but classy, with well-spaced tables and flattering lighting. Awkwardly, we passed Danny at the bar with barely a nod of acknowledgement. We could barely suppress a laugh. Our table was prominently near the center of the busy room. As Danny tells the story, we ordered wine, and he had a word with the waitress—or maybe she was a sommelier—about the fine points of serving us, and that we were from the *Times*. The young lady approached carrying two glasses of white wine on a tray and evidently lost her balance, resulting in a cascade of pinot grigio—or another grape variety—over my chest. Danny could no longer ignore me.

In Venice we wanted to dine at the celebrated Harry's Bar near the Plaza San Marco, where the tipsy specter of Ernest Hemingway, a frequent patron in the 1950s, continues to reel in the tourists. It was foggy and drizzling. We were looking forward to a diverting evening. A host escorted us to one of the best tables in the place, where, dreadfully, depression was waiting in our banquet. What triggered this was unclear. Then again, it was always unclear. First came a headache. My eyes hurt. I felt ghost-like—again, outside of myself. Taped to my refrigerator door today is a black and white photo of Anne and me on the plaza near Harry's, wearing identical trench coats that we had purchased at Saks Fifth Avenue before boarding the *Tuhobic*. My strained smile hardly concealed what was perhaps the worst day of my life. And that is saying a lot.

Being depressed on the road is a special brand of torment. When you are traveling, there are dozens of decisions and requests to make every day, large and small, from choosing where to dine to asking for extra hand towels. Depressed individuals are fearful of communicating with strangers, particularly those who do not share your language. I wanted to go home. But as Winston Churchill is reputed to have said, if you are going through hell, keep going.

What I remember most about Harry's Bar—and I do not remember much—were the brusque, adroit waiters wending through the close dining room, and the aroma of grilling shellfish. We ordered Bellinis, the delicious house cocktail of puréed white peaches and Prosecco, an Italian sparkling wine.

The handsome sitting room, with pale yellow walls, brass sconces, and gleaming wood bar, carried the patina of wealth and style. We sat to the right of the front door, slightly elevated, so as to see and be seen. Perhaps my feeble appearance led them to believe it could be my last meal, and they wanted it to be special. We ordered a seafood risotto, in which the rice was woefully undercooked (al dente is one thing; gravel is another). Pasta with a winey ragù of lamb was luscious, bolstered by a rich lamb stock redolent of fresh rosemary; Anne's bland seafood pasta put the Olive Garden in a favorable light. Our favorite dish was a rich and briny Mediterranean seafood soup made with a flavorful fish stock.

The Bellinis had boosted my spirits somewhat, or at least dialed down the unease, so it was not an altogether lost evening. On the following three days we drove to Rome and the surrounding countryside. Our final stop was to be Florence. On the morning we were packing to leave, the *International Herald Tribune* was delivered to our door. As I was flipping through it a headline caught my eye.

"Oh shit!"

Anne looked up.

"What is it?"

I handed her the paper.

A headline declared: "Best Job in the World Up for Grabs."

The story announced that Mimi Sheraton, the longtime restaurant critic for the *New York Times*, had suddenly resigned. I had a hunch that they would attempt to conscript me for the prestigious position, even though I had been on staff for less than a year. And in my current condition I was definitely not ready for the varsity team. Taking on such a high profile challenge could be my undoing.

I thought it best that we immediately return to New York. Within a few hours of arriving in the newsroom—sick, but not as sick as I was in Venice—I had a sinking feeling about what was coming. The interim restaurant critic was Frank Prial. He urgently wanted off the wine beat in order to return to news as a foreign correspondent.

I received a note saying Arthur Gelb would like to see me at 2:00 p.m. Here it comes.

"Bryan, you know we value you as an exceptional writer."

"Thank you."

"Now that Mimi is gone we have to fill that position, quickly."

"Yes."

"We want to appoint you as restaurant critic."

I had twenty seconds to choose a career: famous *New York Times* dining critic or (depending on how pissed off he would be) copy editor in the matrimonial department. If I had been feeling even 15 percent better that day, the answer might have been different. But it was too much to process for my mud-clogged mind. So I lied, stating that I had been at the *Times* barely nine months, which was intimidating enough, and that having a bright spotlight on my head was more than I cared to experience. And my wife felt the same way.

Gelb was thunderstruck. He had never come across an employee who turned down a big promotion—and a raise. He averred that I would be one of the most prominent bylines at the paper; it would involve cooking, travel, and freedom to write what I pleased. I remained silent. It went on for five strained minutes. Incredulous, Gelb grudgingly let me off the hook. The assignment went to Marian Burros, a first-rate food reporter whose journalistic specialty was health and nutrition. It seemed a mismatch, but I hoped she could pull it off—for her sake as well as mine.

Nine months later, it was obvious that Burros was not happy in the mega-caloric undertaking. Gelb summoned me to his office. I had been feeling marginally better for a few months but not enough to wield the company fork. Once more, I maintained that I was a content employee writing features stories and the Diner's Journal column, a compendium of restaurant news that I had created the previous year. He detonated.

"Do you want to be a star at the *New York Times* or just a reporter?" he huffed. "I am offering you the greatest job in food journalism! You will be the king!"

I was not looking for a coronation; I just wanted to go home and sleep.

He rose and looked out the window toward a marquee for a Broadway play called *A Chorus Line.* He wrenched it open.

"This time I am not asking you," Gelb snarled. "And if you say no again, I will throw you out this goddamn window!"

With a forced smile and firm handshake, I sealed the deal.

There was one more thing.

"Now, when Abe Rosenthal comes in here," Gelb added, "I want you to stand up, shake his hand, and thank him for his confidence in you."

Done.

I returned to my desk and called Anne.

"Get ready. We're restaurant critics."

CHAPTER 16
Missing in Plain Sight

OVERNIGHT MY RESPONSIBILITIES AT THE paper had swelled by a third while my heath remained as erratic as carnival bumper cars. When I was bright and chipper—at that time my illness was cycling roughly every ten days—I continued to labor nonstop, shoveling weeks of editorial coal into the furnace for eight to ten days.

Up to that point, I had not opened up about the depression to anyone at the paper. What was the point? I could have approached Arthur Gelb, but I was not thinking clearly. Impulsively, I resolved to spill it out to one of my editors, Annette Grant, whom I considered a friend. Editor of the Weekend Section, where my column appeared, she was soft spoken and easy going. Surely she would be empathetic and offer some advice. I invited her to lunch at a cozy modern American restaurant on the East Side called Arcadia. A year before I had awarded it two stars. Over a bottle of good white wine and Chesapeake Bay oysters, we first talked shop. Backing into my inquiry, I asked if she found that my work was, well, uneven, that is, from week to week or month to month.

"Well, a little bit," she replied, quizzically.

I opened the sluice gates. The employment interviews, my turning down the restaurant column, struggling to write while cycling. It was a relief, I think. Annette processed it for about fifteen seconds. Her reaction was as terse as it was uncompassionate.

"Why are you telling me this?" she asked. I was so angry and disappointed that it was some years before I opened up to anyone else outside of the family.

On good weeks, I would report and write three restaurant reviews, three Diner's Journal columns, three 60 Minute Gourmet recipe pieces with Pierre Franey and one or two sizable feature stories for the food section. I also recorded three weeks' worth of daily radio commentaries. And that did not count spot news, like a famous chef dropping dead in the meat cooler.

At times the intellectual reverberations in the newsroom were too much for my inert brain, and I had to leave. It has been determined that at any given time, one out of ten Americans suffers from serious depression. I sometimes scanned the newsroom attempting to spot the fallen—but we were too good thespians for that. Every so often, I retreated to the cozy little Gothic library on the tenth floor and sat cross-legged leafing through history books. Or I might descend to the sub-basement, where thunderous printing presses disgorged thousands of newspapers onto waiting trucks—and yes, the papers were "hot off the presses," or at least pretty warm. The main press run was in the evening; in the daytime they ran off special sections.

I had no business being in the pressroom; in fact, it was prohibited. On one of my first visits, I struck up a conversation with a fellow who happened to have grown up near my hometown. After that the crew casually accepted my lugubrious presence. I would sit on a metal staircase and zone out, as in a dream. I did not think about deadlines; I did not think about restaurants. One might wonder: how could I find psychic comfort in a setting that had all the serenity of Yankee Stadium?

As I have mentioned, for me, and I believe for many others so afflicted, time was our nemesis. I could not wait for the day to wind down. During working hours, I fretted about how I was falling behind everyone else. Time moved as slowly as a Bergman film. To speed up the day, when I was not on deadline, I planned mindless diversions.

I often slipped out of the office and circumnavigated squalid Times Square (one reporter dubbed West 43rd Street "Manhattan's largest public urinal"). I began strolling to the East River and back, about a forty-five minute round trip if I did not dawdle. It was a private, almost religious time. (Once I did pray in Saint Patrick's Cathedral.)

At times I felt like the trapped Chilean coal miners, hearing the faint sound of drills yet fretting they could be digging the wrong hole.

One day while walking on the Upper East Side I fell into a situation right out of a Peter Sellers movie. I stumbled, literally, at the entrance to the Spanish Commercial Consulate. As I turned to apologize, a pleasant, nattily dressed man invited me inside. I was in such a fog that I thought perhaps I had met him before. He ushered me into an ornate marble antechamber that led to a large opulent meeting room. There was much hand shaking, and a number of the men called me Mr. Perreti. That was odd, for that is not a Spanish name. And why did they assume I was a Mr. Perreti? As it happens, depressed people are generally very compliant, so I went along with it.

"*Señor*," whispered one of the ushers, "*La mesa a la izquierda.*" (The table on the left.)

I took a seat in front of the place card "Señor Perreti."

White wine, Mr. Perreti?

From the beginning of my illness, I vowed that I would not drink during the day.

"Well, I'll have half a glass, thank you."

Half a glass is not in the Spanish vernacular.

I chatted with several people in passable Spanish, feeling slightly more sociable from the wine. One gentleman was in commercial shipping, another in the olive oil trade. Wonderful platters of tapas were passed around—mussels with green sauce, sizzling shrimp in garlic oil, octopus in vinaigrette, grilled sardines—as the group became more animated. Wine flowed, a flinty white from Galicia. I was surprised that no one asked me about Mr. Perreti's business affairs. It appeared that I was a special guest of some sort. Then something unexpected occurred. A man at a table in front of the room rose, raised a glass, and offered a toast to the organization, followed by another to España. He gazed around the room and lifted his glass again in honor of "three new members of the association." I knew what was coming. I rose along with the other two newcomers and toasted the association, to vigorous applause. But where was the real Mr. Perreti?

It being Iberia, I was certain the luncheon would go on longer than a Bruce Springsteen concert. We moved on to red Rioja wine with the main course: *merluza con salsa verde* (hake, a type of cod, with parsley flaked gelatinous sauce from the Basque called salsa verde, a green sauce). Another round of wine enlivened a slide show on olive production. Halfway through, I politely excused myself, feigning an appointment. It all seemed like a hallucination, albeit an enjoyable one.

As of yet, Dr. Falk's garden variety treatment had yielded just a couple of cherry tomatoes and one eggplant. Conventional medications were proving largely ineffective. In the late 1980s, there arrived a new kid on the block called Prozac, which was ballyhooed as perhaps the greatest depression treatment advance in thirty years, although it had some troublesome side effects including, in rare occasions, suicidal ideations. I found it to be the gentlemen's club of pharmaceuticals, promising complete satisfaction but over time incapable of maintaining psychiatric arousal.

Within a year of its release, Prozac became a popular Pez dispenser not only for the clinically ill but also for people having a bad hair week or who flunked geometry. Critics called it an effective mood stabilizer for many who did not need stabilizing, or for those who would be better served by talk therapy. And what would the world be like without healthy mood fluctuations? Joy. Sadness. Pleasure. Anxiety. Love. Desire. Worry. Prozac can be like belt sanding an antique table—the finished product is smooth and unflawed, but devoid of the burls and crevices that make it unique.

Prozac made me terribly anxious and fatigued, so we put it aside, although it has proven to be highly effective for many patients and is today the most widely prescribed antidepressant in the United States.

When Dr. Liebowitz took over my case, I benefitted from extended stretches of blissful well-being, sometimes as long as a month. There were days that I felt as buoyantly alive as ever. The sky glittered with sapphires; Manhattan assumed a beauty never experienced before; even shit-hole Times Square managed a smile.

I was ingesting a wheel barrow full of medications, more than seventy-five pills a week (It has been as high as 121 a week). Even so, we could not entirely flatten the cycling. It was like Bugs Bunny darting down his rabbit hole and then popping up from another one, and another.

The brutal optimism of new drugs can compound one's woes. Often medications prescribed for one illness can be effective for other maladies as well, even if totally unrelated. Some antidepressants, for example, seem to ameliorate acne. Clozaril, which I took for twenty years, is primarily prescribed for serious schizophrenia. Clearly, I was not schizophrenic. But a dash of it in my pharmaceutical cocktail appeared to help. But Clozaril has one inconvenient side effect, at least for me. One to two hours after taking it I became very drowsy and drifted into sleep, so it had to be ingested at night. Conversely, if I ran out of it, or misplaced it, I would be bug-eyed awake all night.

One day I headed over to the New York Public Library to see a collection of prints from seventeenth century New York City. I must have mistakenly popped several Clozaril before leaving the apartment. Walking along Bryant Park I became very weak and wobbly; I remember clinging to a chest-high stone wall and unsuccessfully attempting to crawl over it and onto some grass. Two people came over and attempted to prop me up but my legs gave way, and I fell onto the pavement. A cop arrived and looked down at me. He spoke, but I could not reply. Within minutes an ambulance arrived, and by that time I had nearly passed out. My next recollection was awakening

in the emergency room of the Weill Cornell Medical Center on East
68th Street.

After a long, restorative nap, I explained to a doctor what had happened. He suggested I stay put for a couple of hours as the drug wore
off. When he learned I was a restaurant critic, he summoned two colleagues—presumably their patients were not in critical condition—for
an ad hoc tutorial on Manhattan dining.

"Where would you go for great Italian food? Not too expensive, not
too noisy, not too far from the hospital."

"Chinatown. Your favorite three Chinese places!"

"Steakhouses. Best steakhouses?"

I hopped a cab for the Upper West Side, arriving just in time to
meet my dining guests at the upscale Shun Lee Palace. I did not mention the hospital detour.

Around that time, I was put in touch with a Dr. Richard Raskin, an
esteemed and likeable psychotherapist who headed the Pace University counselling center. It was evident that drugs alone were not going
to pull me back onto the boat, so I was to begin seeing him twice a
week. That two-prong assault would drain our finances. Anne continued with freelance work. Still, the therapies left little discretionary
income. Health insurance at the time did not cover psychotherapy,
which was scandalous. Psychopharmacology was a different matter,
and was covered up to 80 percent. I was in such a muddled state of
mind, however, that I never applied for it, losing out on tens of thousands of dollars over the years.

CHAPTER 17
First Review

WHERE SHOULD I GO FOR my first restaurant review? The world was waiting. One of the hot new American places would be timely; Italian restaurants, traditionally stodgy and red-sauced, were improving steadily; a casual French bistro might do it. No, I reasoned, there will be time for all of those. Think off the grid.

I elicited the assistance of my secretary, Velma Cannon, as we researched interesting new places. Velma had been secretary to the paper's first restaurant critic, Craig Claiborne, for more than twenty-five years. Craig was a globe-trotting celebrity with a massive expense account and a byzantine sex life. Like Beaver Cleaver, he was always getting into fixes—drunken driving arrests, travel snafus, romantic complications—and Velma was there to bail him out. She always said she had "three helpless sons" (along with me and Pierre). I cannot say how many times Velma came to my rescue, when I would go to a restaurant without my credit card—the paper arranged for cards with different names every year or so—or sprint out the door forgetting what restaurant I was reviewing.

Attractive, stylish, and with a girlish, trilling laugh, Velma had seen it all. Prior to the 1960s, African Americans in the newsroom were required to hold college degrees. Whites were not. Velma had graduated from Hampton University, in Hampton, Virginia, near the Chesapeake Bay. It is a traditionally black institution founded in 1868 to provide education to newly freed African Americans. She was proud of her school, and well into her eighties she attended class reunions and sorority gatherings. It was a measure of my wretched self-absorption that I never asked her about Hampton University and her time there. In fact, I know virtually nothing about her family, outside of her daughter, Jill, nor where she grew up nor how she came to reside in New York City. She mentioned on occasion her deceased husband, named Corky. He remains a mystery as well.

It was more than ironic that the one person in the newsroom who least desired someone to talk with all day long had a fulltime assistant. Frankly, whether well or ill, I did not know what to do with a secretary. I came up the small newspaper route. At my first job I shared a phone. Now I had a college graduate clipping my articles and making restaurant reservations.

When I was depressed and uncommunicable, I sat, inert, in my cubicle adjacent to Velma's. I did nothing. She did nothing. Every hour or so I moped over to make small talk. I wanted to keep her busy as part of the news operation, but I was too ill to reach out—and when I once asked if she would like to help me with some research, she said no. And looking back, it seems absurd that in the ten years we worked together I was unsure if she was aware of my illness—even though she once accompanied me in an ambulance when I accidently overdosed on medication. I never confided in her nor apologized for being a negligent boss.

When Velma was in her mid-nineties, I paid her a visit at her apartment in Chelsea, where Jill was spending much of her time. By then my depression was behind me and in a strange sense it was like meeting her anew. I wanted to tell her everything about my life. I wanted to ask her everything about her family and Hampton University and Corky and her life outside of the *Times*. Concerning my affliction, I imagine she would have laughed, waved her hand, and said, "I know everything about my boys." She asked about my son. I had promised to bring him over when he was about four, but never did, and I do not know why. I asked if she remembered the day I was rolled out of the newsroom on a gurney.

"Oh yes," she said. "I rode in the ambulance. You were in bad shape." How strange that we never discussed it. I suppose it was my responsibility to bring it up. What an oral history I could have recorded. It was just one of so many opportunities denied me by the disease.

One day in a taxi, I drove by a crazy looking restaurant on West Broadway, in Tribeca, called El Internacional. It resembled a 1950s nightclub designed by Antoni Gaudí. The curvaceous white façade was studded with colored glass, and on the roof was an eight-foot-high Statue of Liberty. Perfect.

Sitting at my desk two days before my first visit to El Internacional to review it, I spotted Abe Rosenthal shambling across the newsroom in my direction. Normally, that would be reason to crawl under the desk—what did I do wrong? He stopped and asked, "Bryan, what is your first restaurant going to be?" I told him, and said I had not yet dined there, but planned to go soon. Luckily, I was enjoying a sound stretch of health and greatly looked forward to it.

The following day Abe stopped by again.

"I went to El Internacional last night," he said. "I won't tell you what I think, but it's worth writing up."

My guests on that maiden voyage were longtime friends Bernhard and Victoria Horstmann. He grew up in Germany and Hong Kong and was in the wine trade; she was from Argentina and in the advertising business. I suppose I should have been nervous. To be sure, the editor-heavy *Times* would be passing the review around the newsroom. But as I was feeling so well and confident that evening, I was ready to take them on.

The bustling bar was lined with subway tiles trimmed in gold. The dining rooms were decidedly un-Iberian, with the larger space done in surreal clashing colors with red-flocked wallpaper.

El Internacional featured one of the first, if not *the* first, tapas bars in the city. Having lived in Spain, I could attest to the food's authenticity:

baby mushrooms in sherry sauce, grilled squid, codfish with eggplant and peppers, Spanish tortilla, grilled sardines, and more.

If there is a quintessential Catalan dish, it is duck with pears, and there it was prepared magnificently. The huge braised duck leg was served in a semisweet sauce of pureed pears with tomato, onions, and carrots. It was garnished with a poached pear half. The other nightly special was poached red snapper in a bright lime-butter sauce with shallots. It tasted better than it sounded. I was startled to see on the menu angulas, the tiny freshwater eels from Spain that Anne and I had sampled on our first evening together in Salamanca. Traditionally, they are served in an earthenware crock with sizzling oil and garlic. There they were swathed in hot sauce, which was good, but it muted the flavor of the eels.

In the 1980s, Spanish cuisine was not a showcase for desserts. El Internacional served a perfect *crèma Catalana* (a *crème brûlée*), silky and rich inside, with a seared brittle sugar crust. Guava pudding, which had a soft bready texture, could have used more guava. Cheese selections in New York restaurants were relatively paltry at the time—mostly French, a little Spanish, and some American goat cheeses. At El Internacional, they served a familiar Catalan combination of sharp aged goat cheese with pine nuts and honey. I recall scraping up a final taste of the luscious *crèma Catalana* and thinking to myself, "They're going to pay me to do this?"

I awarded El Internacional two stars.

CHAPTER 18
Food Revolution

IT WOULD NOT BE AN overstatement to say that the 1980s and 1990s were the golden age of food journalism, a time of unmatched gastronomic invention and discovery. I happened to arrive at the party just as the table was set and the menus presented. In late 1984, when the role of *Times* restaurant critic was bestowed (forced) upon me, there were virtually no weekly dining columnists in the city, save the stylish and entertaining Gael Green at *New York* magazine. The Zagat Survey, in which diners rated restaurants and the results were printed in a guide, was just gaining traction. That state of affairs invested in me inordinate power; too much power one could argue, and certainly much more than today's major critics, who compete with the hundreds of self-appointed bloggers who infest the web. Every Thursday night, around 9:30 p.m., a gaggle of restaurant owners assembled in the *Times*' lobby awaiting the first edition of the paper to see if they had been reviewed (At the time restaurant reviews appeared on Fridays). At the designated time, an ink-smudged printer arrived and placed an armful of papers in the news box.

"We carried a lot of quarters in those days, " recalls Drew Nieporant, of the Myriad Restaurant Group.

Such was the hunger for restaurant news that I sometimes wrote two reviews a week plus an expanded Diner's Journal column. With that, and my other writing responsibilities for the food section, speed was of the essence (again, my AP training came in handy). In writing my columns, I was not trying to be Flaubert, but rather a reliable source of consumer information presented in a readable and entertaining fashion.

The *Times* created its stand-alone food and wine section in 1975, prompting newspapers around the country to do the same. Craig Claiborne became the paper's food editor in 1957, and shortly thereafter launched a restaurant column that is credited with having invented the genre. Drool-worthy culinary magazines sprouted, like *Food and Wine* and *Bon Appétit*. Food TV came along about ten years later— the Emeril-ization of America. Many people, even those who rarely cooked in their vanity kitchens, became addicted to cooking shows and cookbooks.

I maintained a casual relationship with Claiborne. He was soft-spoken, even shy, and always very cordial with me. In subsequent years, I learned that he was an enthusiastic supporter of my work, and was personally responsible for my promotion to restaurant critic.

For the upward strata of Manhattanites in the 1980s dining out evolved from sustenance to social statement. There were so many noteworthy new restaurants coming on line that I could barely keep up. Thanks to the churning food press, culinarians became household names: Daniel Boulud (Le Cirque), Gilbert Le Coze (Le Bernardin), David Bouley (Bouley), Susan and Barry Wine (the Quilted Giraffe), Charley Palmer (Aureole), Jean Georges Vongerichten (Lafayette), Alfred Portale (Gotham Bar and Grill), Larry Forgione (the River Café), and more. It was heavy freight for a food writer who, only three years before, had been writing about *pasta puttanesca* in Bridgeport.

When I was at the *Journal Inquirer*, every Friday on the way to work I would stop at a convenience store to buy the *New York Times* and read the restaurant review by Mimi Sheraton. I never dreamed I would assume that position one day—at that time I had yet to write a single food article—nor any role at the *Times*. I simply enjoyed reading the deftly written articles, especially when she disassembled some overrated restaurant, leaving its windows blown out and fragments of dishes on the sidewalk.

I was fortunate to have arrived in New York City as the starting gun popped for the so-called American Food Revolution. Fewer than ten years before, fine dining in the city was French dining, with sumptuous redoubts like La Grenouille, La Côte Basque, Lutèce, Le Périgord, Le Chantilly, La Caravelle, Le Normand, and others. There existed only a handful of distinctive American establishments like the Four Seasons, the Coach House, Forum of the Twelve Caesars, and Windows on the World.

Shortly after New York City burrowed out of its self-inflicted financial crisis of the mid-1970s, the food and dining scene exploded. People had money and they were more adventuresome travelers. Entrepreneurs could avail themselves of reasonable interest rates; commercial rents were affordable. Cuisinarts and pasta makers flew out of Zabar's and Bloomingdale's. Urban farmers' markets took root, the organic movement flourished, cookbooks cascaded onto the scene, and home wine cellars were the ultimate symbol of urbanity and wealth. "Gourmet" was the adjective of the decade—she is a "gourmet" cook, and they have a "gourmet" kitchen where they are learning to cook with "gourmet" ingredients.

The city's near bankruptcy spooked many of Manhattan's corporations, causing them to click off the lights and relocate to the suburbs and beyond. They left behind real estate like lofts and storefronts ripe for gentrification. Among these neighborhoods—believe it or not—were Soho, Tribeca, Chelsea, and the Upper West Side. When I started reviewing, in 1984, I resolved to find one restaurant in each borough outside of Manhattan. In Brooklyn, I dined at the historic steakhouse Peter Luger, the River Café, and the classic American Gage and Tollner, but that was about it. As for Queens and the Bronx—virtually nothing for my readers. Don't even ask about Staten Island.

Before and during that time, young Americans apprenticed in fine restaurants or attended cooking schools like the Culinary Institute of America and Johnson & Wales. A number of these novices went to France in order to toil at the aprons of culinary titans like Paul Bocuse, Roger Verge, Café, Alain Chapel, and the brothers Troigros. Some of the young Francophiles trained in the discipline of *nouvelle* cuisine, in which classic flour-thickened sauces gave way to lighter reductions, fanciful presentations, and pristine ingredients.

The year 1986 was, in my experience, the launch pad for some remarkably diverse and seminal restaurants whose influences are palpable even today. Never had so many outstanding establishments opened in one year. I wrote highly favorable reviews of Le Bernardin, Lafayette, Union Square Cafe, Aurora, Palio, Jams, Rosa Mexicano, and the Quilted Giraffe (three of which exist today). It was more than a dining transformation; it was a gastronomic insurgency.

Unlike French cuisine, with its familiar and predictable menus, new American restaurants were surprising and exploratory. Looking over my first book (*The New York Times Guide to Restaurants in New York City*), I saw mention of a cozy American place on East 22nd Street called Hubert's. Owned by a young American couple, Karen and Len Allison, it served items like herb-flecked grilled rabbit sausage with mole sauce, and titillated with seafood like steamed fluke with ginger broth (Japanese influences cannot be overstated). Gotham Bar and Grill, in the West Village, came out with dishes like sautéed Norwegian salmon atop a mound of spinach with grilled fennel, and a shallot-and-saffron custard. Grilling became the rage with the arrival of a sunny, boisterous place called Jams, which sparked the California grilling craze.

Manhattan had many Italian establishments, but virtually all were of the checked tablecloth variety, not places one would go for a night on the town.

"When I arrived in New York there were no real Italian restaurants," Danny Meyer, of the Union Square Hospitality Group, told me. "They were either red sauce style or on the higher level imitation French."

Upscale Italian restaurants meekly mimicked the French, with ornate dining rooms, waiters in black tie, French wine lists, fine tableware, and the most lavish flower arrangements this side of the Rose Bowl. Many of the menus were interchangeable with those of the French. You would find Gallic-style fare anchored by rich sauces like *béchamel, hollandaise, espagnole,* and *Chantilly,* most of which were bound with wheel barrows of cream and butter. Of course, today, Italian food, particularly that at casual trattorias, is by far the most popular cuisine in the city.

As far back as Craig Claiborne, who started the dining column in 1959, the paper has used a rating system from one to four stars (and the embarrassing "satisfactory" or "poor"). My ratings were calculated roughly as 75 percent for food and wine, and 25 percent for service and ambiance. Typically, we were four diners, so at three dishes per guest—I often ordered more—it came out to a minimum of twelve dishes per visit, or thirty-six plus dishes per review. (And a lot of food sharing.) My bottomless expense account allowed for as many visits as necessary. While three was generally adequate, there were occasions when I went five or six times—or, in the case of the four star French seafood restaurant Le Bernardin, eight times.

Being a bushwhacker from rural New Jersey, I was ill at ease spending hundreds of dollars a day on food and drink. A number of times I inquired of my superiors if my expense account had an off switch. (My guess was that I spent around $125,000 a year, in New York City alone). My pockets were swollen with cash and credit cards. Whenever Anne and I traveled out of town or overseas, VISA contacted us, concerned we had been abducted and relieved of our credit cards. The subway rarely saw our feet. Several times I posed the expense account question to Warren Hoge, who at the time was an assistant managing editor in charge of personnel.

"Look at it this way, Bryan," he explained. "We have a correspondent in Nairobi. To keep him there costs, say, $125,000. Now we get a hell of a bigger bang for the buck with you. Don't worry." I took him to dinner.

My approach to assigning stars differed from that of my successors. For one, I did not go in for silly disguises. Frequently, and embarrassingly, they do not work. What is more, they are unnecessary. When I worked at Restaurant du Village, critics would occasionally come in. I looked at the chef and asked, "what do we do?" There was little we could do, for when a restaurant opens for service the ingredients are prepped and the sauce bases are ready to go. I suppose you could serve the critics a bigger steak or ring the plate with caviar. As I mentioned, for the *Times*, I tasted forty or more dishes before writing. You cannot fake that.

Another issue is preferential treatment in the dining room. Some critics get all frothed up if another table seems to be receiving extra attention. That never offended me. Restaurants are not democratic institutions, they are businesses. Like other businesses—a wine store, a repair shop, a dry cleaner—the best customers may deserve special treatment. At the same time, *all* diners deserve a certain high level of service. If some regular customers are coddled, get over it.

I must admit that on the occasions I was recognized I received every courtesy short of a neck massage. In those cases, I assessed the service by observing other tables.

As far as writing was concerned, I strove to be clear, direct, authoritative, and enjoyable to read. If you look over my columns, you will find that in virtually every one there is a fillip of humor, a play on words, a funny metaphor, or simile. That was not by accident. My intention was to make readers smile at least once and give them something to remember. All writers want to be remembered. Recently I was introduced to a music producer and ardent foodie who had followed my column in the nineties. He recalled some favorite dining spots that I had recommended, and added that, at the same time, he always looked forward to the "smile sentence." He may not have remembered specific dishes, he said, but he looked forward to my editorial tidbit.

"I'll tell you one I remember," he told me. "You wrote that waiters at a new restaurant were more nervous than a long-tailed cat in a roomful of rocking chairs. Hah!"

CHAPTER 19
How to Review a Restaurant when Depressed

FOR STARTERS, MY ADVICE IS: do not review a restaurant when depressed. Unless, of course, you are being remunerated for the service and have little choice. It can be done all right, but like rutabagas, if you have an alternative, take it. The first obstacle in restaurant reviewing when depressed is summoning the strength to pass through the door. By entering the establishment you are irretrievably committing to more than two hours of socializing, at times with people you hardly know and who are elated to be there and have a million questions about how reviewing is done. I usually paused outside of the restaurant to dispense a measure of self-therapy. I would close my eyes and try to reassure myself that I could do it, however excruciating it might be, and that it would pass quickly. What is more, returning home would not alleviate the pain, and would most likely sharpen it because of guilt. And I had nothing in the fridge.

On that particular evening, en route to a buoyant restaurant near my apartment, on the Avenue of the Americas, I encountered someone whose life was, in a way, as arduous as mine. In the late 1970s, with New York City still mired in a sinkhole of debt, there appeared on the streets of New York a heartbreaking representation of failed social services and tepid community indifference: the bag lady. Many in their sixties or older, these silent, un-emotive waifs, wearing tatty housecoats and blank expressions, propelled grocery carts filled to the brim with plastic bags of clothes and God knows what else. There was no pan-handling; no peddling; no crazy talk. In fact, bag ladies were nearly invisible, urban wraiths who largely wanted to be left alone.

I paused at the restaurant door longer than usual and then backed away toward Sixth Avenue, where I nearly collided with a grocery cart. The diminutive gray-haired woman hesitated to make eye contact. She appeared to be in her seventies, and looked clean and well nourished.

"Hi," I said.

"Hello," she whispered, gazing at the sidewalk.

I had no suitable follow-up question. What could I say, "Where are you going?"

I told her I was having dinner at the restaurant and needed to get some air.

"I was a cook," she said, but when I asked where she had no answer. She seemed to have trouble enunciating. On a finger was a ring; it looked like a wedding band. I was going to ask her name but chose to respect her privacy.

"I cooked in the Poconos," she said.

"Hah," I said. "Honeymoon capital of America! Or it used to be."

She nodded.

"I don't want to go in there," I said, gesturing toward the restaurant.

She flashed me a look of bemusement. Who would not want to go in there?

"I have to go now," she said; enough conversation for one evening. She battened down her cargo and ambled down the avenue, silently, purposefully, as if on the way to a business meeting.

We each walked with our silent demons. One could say that I was merely a well-dressed bag lady, plodding through day after murky day while attempting to draw as little attention as possible.

Arriving at the table I would act upbeat, hospitable, even voluble. At times I invited two couples to join me in order to sample as much food as possible.

One might presume that after doing it so many times, the exercise would be more tolerable. But no. Depression gives no quarter, and never misses an opportunity to corrupt a good time. It was my first visit to China Grill, a vast, thunderous spot that occupied an entire block between 52nd and 53rd Streets in what was referred to as the CBS "Black Rock" tower.

That evening my recruits were old friends Avi Sharir and Louise Gerson. They were usually eager to join me and available. As a rule, the worse I felt, the more selective I became with dining partners. With a six night a week (and three lunches) eating schedule, it was not uncommon to run out of dining guests, in which case I might troll the newsroom in search of overworked and undernourished journalists. All dining critics should have in their wallets the phone numbers of friends who are such ardent diners they would interrupt a colonoscopy to arrive on time. Foremost was my friend Glenn Dopf, a renowned medical defense attorney in Manhattan and a spectacular trencherman. Tall and amiable, he probably dined out as much as I did entertaining clients nearly every day. He had a discerning palate, and could hurdle through three main courses and four or five desserts without breaking a sweat. One evening he dined with Jacques Torres, a renowned pastry chef, at an Italian restaurant on the Upper West Side. An Italian cuisine aficionado, Glenn asked the waiter how many types of pasta were available.

"Twenty five," he replied.

"Bring all of them," Glenn beamed.

He did. And they consumed them—albeit cheating a bit, with half portions.

Avi and Louise had come down from Demarest, New Jersey, about twenty minutes north of Manhattan. Louise was a classmate of mine at Columbia University's Graduate School for Journalism and a producer at NBC News. (At school, students produced documentaries on the theme of living in New York. Louise made a film about bag ladies.) Petite, risible, and quick-witted, she was a dead ringer for Joan Rivers. The quintessential Jewish mother, she was an Olympic worrier. Every couple of weeks I could expect a call from Louise checking to see if I were dead. And, along with my mother, she was the only person who consistently inquired if I was getting enough to eat. Though Avi and Louise inhabited my inner orbit, I did not believe they were aware of my situation, or at least the seriousness of it. If I could fool Louise, I could fool anyone. And I believe, like many depressed individuals, I *did* conceal it well both at work and among friends.

As F. Scott Fitzgerald said of his character Dick Diver: "The façade can remain intact after the interior has crumbled—and that a clear eye and a steady voice can stand guard over a seriously disintegrating personality."

I have searched the psychiatric literature for information linking depression and anxiety with taste disorders. It is a nascent field, and one of the first disciplined studies was conducted back in 2006 by a researcher named Lucy Donaldson, of Nottingham University, in England. Her inquiry suggested that two neurotransmitters associated with mood can, when abnormally low, cause changes in taste perception. The team tested healthy participants for sensitivity before and after taking antidepressants that boosted levels of these neurotransmitters. When the subjects had enhanced serotonin levels, they were 27 percent more sensitive to sucrose, and quinine tasted 53 percent more bitter. And with heightened noradrenaline levels, bitterness was perceived as stronger, while sensitivity to sourness increased by 22 percent. That does not shed a whole lot of light on the topic, but it is interesting to consider. My taste buds were reliable and conscientious employees, never once letting me down.

Getting back to my dinner companions that night: Avi was a thin, knotty, animated fellow of a jocular disposition. An Israeli, he had commanded a tank in the previous Arab war. He and Louise had been married for eight years. Their son, Nathaniel, came into the world hobbled by a hideous disorder called familial dysautonomia. For the first year of his life, Louise called me to complain, exasperated, "This kid won't eat." Two pediatricians dismissed Louise's concerns, saying that it was not unusual and that she should stop overreacting.

The exceedingly rare disease, typically found in Jews from a certain part of Eastern Europe, carries a backpack of debilitating and life-shortening symptoms: the complete absence of hunger, an inability to chew and swallow, stunted growth, lack of reactions to heat and pain, and more. Few of the afflicted live to their college years. The heartbreaking stress of raising their child contributed to the dissolution of their marriage. Louise confided to me that she was upset because she had to shoulder 90 percent of the demanding child care, and cut short her career, while Avi had virtually washed his hands of the situation.

China Grill was, like China, huge. Its two vast dining rooms under a thirty-foot-ceiling were linked by a long bar facing the frenzied cooking stations. If there were a contest for the loudest restaurant in New York City, China Grill would certainly be a finalist. It was designed to be loud: marble walls, marble floors, a soaring ceiling, overpopulated rooms, and a huge open kitchen of flaring woks.

The mid-1980s was the zenith of big, brash, theatrical restaurants. For twenty-somethings, dining out was not just part of an evening on the town; it *was* an evening on the town. One-stop shopping. In a gambit to sate these desires, restaurateurs created massive dining Pamplonas with hundreds of seats, casual menus, and runway-length bars. One of the more amusing was the stadium-sized restaurant called America, in the East Village, which had 350 seats. The menu carried 160 selections. Happily, it was a short-lived fad.

My first observation was that China Grill's kitchen was bereft of Chinese people or Asians of any sort. That was not surprising. In 90 percent of Manhattan restaurants, it is Latinos—principally Mexicans and Central Americans—who tow the barge, from peeling carrots to preparing the most elegant entrees. Like a Detroit assembly line, everyone has a confined and repetitive task. In top-tier establishments there may be an "executive chef," formerly known as the "chef," whose function is to expedite (inspect finished dishes before they leave the kitchen) or, if he is a "celebrity chef," troll the dining room, fishing for compliments.

I had eaten at China Grill once before and was impressed. The food was sparkling fresh, eye-catching, creative, healthful, and well-priced. Wines were well matched to the food and affordable.

My dining protocol went like this:

Visit one: Guests can order anything on the menu as long as there are no duplications.

Visit two: Guests may order anything on the menu pending my approval.

Visit three: Eat what I tell you.

A grilled squab was excellent, crisp-skinned, mildly gamey, and with a caramelized black vinegar sauce that delivered a ying-yang sensation of sweet and sharp. Equally good was a honey-glazed duck with parchment-thin skin and a semi-sweet plum sauce. I always ordered a number of extra dishes in order to sample as much as possible.

I managed to have a pleasant evening, catching up on families, work, and friends. There was one more topic of conversation that Louise always brought up: Match making. Louise derived great pleasure in match-making. Being divorced and a restaurant critic, I was on her A list. But at that moment I was a wallflower in the school gym. Depression medications have numerous side effects aside from hand tremors, like dry mouth, fatigue, teeth grinding, even irritability. Louise's sorority had a number of attractive candidates—a Harvard law student, a TV producer, a college professor. I did not believe I would be a great catch for any of them. It was not worth the embarrassment.

In 2000, Louise underwent surgery for breast cancer. Characteristically, she kept up a plucky front, joking as if it were a Joan Rivers monologue. In the ensuing two years we dined every several months or so, with her new husband, Tom. There was a second surgery.

All appeared to go well for a year.

On a sunny fall day shortly before Halloween, Louise called.

She sounded uncharacteristically measured, matter of fact.

"They found more tumors. This time in the brain," she said.

How does one respond to that?

"Maybe the lasers can zap them?" I knew lasers could not zap them.

"There are too many."

In the ensuing weeks Louise continued to call *me* to make sure *I* was alive.

The last time we spoke, Louise confessed that for two years she had been aware of my struggles but had chosen not to intrude at the moment.

"How did you learn about it?" I asked.

"I'm an investigative journalist," she laughed. "I called your sister!"

Weeks went by. I was unsure if I should go to Louise's house or just leave her in peace. The fact that she had ceased calling signaled things were dire. I drove up to the house. There were no cars in the driveway so I walked around to the kitchen window, startling the housekeeper.

"They all went to the city," she said. "I think at this point she wants privacy."

There was a final phone call. Her voice was hoarse but otherwise appeared strong. She said she loved me.

Before hanging up, she summoned the real Louise and said in a clear maternal tone:

"I know how difficult it has been to work on your book," she said. "But don't stop, even if you have to do one page a day. Do it for me."

"I will."

"And if you DON'T do it, I'll come back and haunt you!"

CHAPTER 20
Dining With...

I TURNED DOWN A DINNER with Paul Newman and Joanne Woodward. Think about how detached from western civilization one must be to do that. I had nearly forgotten about the incident until recently when I was researching this book and came across the following handwritten note.

> *Dear Bryan.*
> *We look forward to dining with you soon. Hope all is well.*
> *Best,*
> *Paul and Joanne*

There is a back story to that episode. In 1988, the Newmans, great humanitarians and philanthropists, founded the Hole in the Wall Gang Camp, in pastoral Ashford, Connecticut. It was (and still is) dedicated to providing summer fun and educational activities to children with serious diseases like cancer and multiple sclerosis. It is a marvelous program, with horseback riding, water sports, games, a professional theater, arts and crafts, and much more. To a visitor it is an inspiring place, and a heartbreaking place.

Every summer the camp puts on a big variety show in the theater featuring some of the kids, as well as many of the Newmans' renowned friends—actors, musicians, artists, writers. At the time I played guitar in a Cajun/Zydeco band. Because of my celebrity in the world of gastronomy, we played food and wine festivals around the country. Paul Newman, or someone on his staff, heard about us and asked if we would perform at the camp. It was a wonderful experience, and I believe the kids got a kick out of it.

Some months later I received a call from Joanne, a lovely person, inviting me to a cocktail and buffet affair at their apartment on Fifth Avenue. I gladly accepted. That happened to be one of those exhausting weeks between depression cycles and I was working twelve hour days. Still, when Butch Cassidy and his girl call, you perk up. It was a small affair, maybe a dozen guests. I brought along a friend, Jodi, who worked in the publicity department of the March of Dimes. When we entered the apartment some of the guests looked vaguely familiar. In the corner, next to a grand piano, a quartet played classical music. Not just any quartet, it was the first violinist from the New York Philharmonic and three other "firsts."

I settled onto a couch next to a gentleman that I definitely had seen before: Sydney Poitier. He was friendly, on the quiet side, and radiated class. The apartment, which afforded a panoramic view of Central Park, was quite warm. Very warm. I dared not remove my suit jacket unless Sydney did so first. A circulating butler took drink orders, and we availed ourselves of a buffet in the dining room. The combination of heat, alcohol, food, fatigue, and lulling music left me conspicuously drowsy. Jodi, who was seated at the opposite side of the room, faced me, wide eyed, and mimed, "D-O-N-T ... F-A-L-L ... A-S-L-E-E-P!"

By Jodi's estimate, I dozed for nearly five minutes. Of course, upon awakening, I was mortified. But that was not the half of it. Most of my recuperative nap took place on the broad shoulder of Mr. Poitier. I lifted my head ever so slowly, as if he would not notice. The other guests surely observed my performance. Sydney never mentioned it. Nor did the Newmans. Jodi assured me that—thank God—I did not snore.

Embarrassed, I sent the Newmans a thank you note and, as a casual gesture, invited them to join me on a restaurant review someday.

Several weeks later I received a hand written card from the couple taking me up on the offer. At that time, I was experimenting with yet another new regimen of medications. These left me trembling even more, to the degree I could not hold a wine glass nor lift food from plate to mouth. I bought some time lying that I would be going to Spain for a month to research a book (that was 20 percent true).

A month later the tremors had not abated. Two months went by. Three months. I could not take the chance of having them think I had Parkinson's disease, or was an alcoholic. By that time I was too ashamed to call them, and lie. I was so tired of lying.

In 1991 I created a column for the food section called Dining With. The idea was to invite notable people to dinner, usually those with an interest in restaurants and cooking. Conversation would be about food and family, not their careers, which they were asked about all the time. Among my roster: Dolly Parton, Stephen King, Pavoratti, Yves Montand, Martina Navratilova, Ray Davies, Garrison Keillor, and Malcomb Forbes.

It was a risky endeavor, considering my cycling. My first date was with one of the nicest and most uplifting people I have ever met: Dolly Parton. She suggested we meet at an old line steakhouse in the Broadway Theater district called Wally and Joseph's.

I had a thrumming headache, no doubt the result of a new medication, and was perspiring abundantly. Upon arriving, Dolly did not exactly melt into the crowd: Fifty percent blonde mane, 30 percent bust, and the rest a twiggy support system that kept her at a kinetic pace.

Dolly was in town to promote her latest film, called Straight Talk. It revolved around her experiences in the pressured world of big-city news media. "It was an easy character for me because I wasn't really acting," she said. "That's really me." She wore a black bodysuit, yellow and black stiletto heels, rings the size of crystal paperweights, and a canary-yellow waist-length jacket embroidered with black Country Western curlicues.

Dolly greeted more than a dozen diners, not in a detached celebrity manner, but as if she would like to join them if she were not tied up with a reporter. She even slid into a black leather banquette with four ladies who were in town to see a play.

Dolly finally sat down at our table.

"Hey, you feelin' okay, honey?" asked the queen of country music.

"It's fine, I just have a little headache."

"Oh, that's too bad. You want me to run out and get some aspirin?"

Now, stop reading this book for a moment. Close your eyes, and imagine Dolly Parton, in full Grand Ole Opry raiment, sashaying into an over-illuminated CVS and asking for the pain relief aisle. Rattle that around in your brain for a while.

She ordered a white wine spritzer.

"I usually order a tequila right away," she said. "You see, I don't like the taste of alcohol all that much, so I have a shot of tequila to get a quick buzz on." A high-pitched laugh.

Dolly declared that she never doubted she would make it to Nashville. "I graduated from high school on a Friday night in 1964," she recalled. "On Saturday morning I left for Nashville, never to come back."

She ordered her favorite appetizer: chopped clams casino. "I like clams but I don't like them when they're all big and chewy, so they chop them up for me," she said as the waiter took an order for two portions. She then asked for a baked potato and a salad with ranch dressing. "That's it," she said. "Just give me my potato, any kind of potato, and I'm happy."

Dolly, who volunteered that she was five feet two inches tall and 110 pounds, said she loves to eat, but that potatoes have been her dietary Waterloo.

"Every single diet I ever fell off of was because of potatoes and gravy of some sort," she said. "That's partly how I got into trouble a few years back. My career was getting very successful and I was going to all of these events where you eat and drink and sit on your backside. I had to lose forty-five pounds after that."

Dolly said her early experiences formed habits that are hard to shake. It took her years to eat a lot of shellfish. "I was probably twenty years old before I had even seen a shrimp cocktail. I like oysters, but fried. The only things we had at home were frog legs, river fish, and catfish. And it was almost always fried."

My headache was gone—the curative power of Dolly's persona.

She mentioned she is a meat eater. "In the Smoky Mountain National Park there were a lot of migrating bears," she said. "My father and my uncles were big bear hunters, and they had bear dogs. We ate a lot of bear, rabbit, squirrel, and groundhog. See, we were country people, and when you grow up in the mountains you grow up eating whatever's running around."

She proclaimed her chopped clams a smashing success. "Do you like 'em?" she asked. "This way you get the flavor of the clams and bread crumbs all mixed up."

The salad was fine, too, but, alas, the baked potato never arrived. "I guess they forgot," she whispered so her friend the waiter wouldn't hear. She would rather go without her main course than upset her friend.

Her favorite meal for entertaining is roast pork, green beans, turnip greens, and fried okra. She likes red wine, and, she added, prefers those with a little dryish feeling at the end, from wood aging. "With my fair skin and everything, when I drink a few glasses I start to turn all red!"

Her startlingly long, shiny red fingernails could double as supermarket coffee scoops, which prompted me to ask the question, "How can you play guitar with those nails?"

Dolly did not miss a beat. "Damnnn gooood," she drawled, bursting into laughter.

CHAPTER 21
Mireille

JOHN STEINBECK MAINTAINED THAT AN autobiography that does not reveal something disgraceful is not to be trusted. Looking over a life marked by moral impoverishment on my part, this memoir would easily earn the great writer's approval. That my misbehavior was rooted in the toxic sink hole of depression may be somewhat exculpatory, maybe not. If there is any consolation, the two most important women in my life, Anne and Mireille (whom you are about to meet) as well as the two most damaged, understand the narrative and have forgiven me. We remain in close touch.

Owing to my exotic and high profile newspaper beat, I was somewhat of a celebrity in the newsroom. I could drop by editors' offices for a chat or to tender a dinner invitation. The top brass stopped by my desk for dining advice. One day I received a call from Abe Rosenthal's secretary. She informed me that Mr. Rosenthal would be dining at Le Cirque the following evening in the company of Beverly Sills, a famous operatic soprano. At the time, Le Cirque, on East 65th Street, was the most chic and exclusive restaurant in the city, perhaps the country. It was Manhattan's ultimate society fish bowl, and one's rank in the celebrity status depended to a large degree on your relationship with owner Sirio Maccioni. It was the most electrifying dining room I had ever seen. Celebrities, yes, from Woody Allen to Yves Montand to the king of Spain. Yet the place exuded such imperturbable class that it did not feel like a celebrity establishment. No one stared; no one asked for an autograph. Pierre brought me there for lunch shortly after we began working together. He ordered fettuccine with cream sauce and white truffles. I had never tasted truffles. It was a mind-altering, sensual experience.

Evidently Rosenthal had misgivings about the reception he would receive in full view of the soignée patrons. No doubt Beverly Sills would receive the full Maccioni treatment: a gushing "*bon soir*," the fond embrace, the pecking of cheeks, the strategic introductions.

"Mr. Rosenthal," the secretary explained, somewhat sheepishly. "He would ... uh, well, would you mind calling the owner of Le Cirque and make him aware of who Mr. Rosenthal is?"

Unbelievable. The executive editor of the *New York Times*, whose photo had appeared in the press dozens of times, was insecure because he feared that Maccioni would swoon over Ms. Sills and treat him like a professional escort?

I had no business calling restaurant owners and asking for favors. It was clearly a conflict of interest.

"Sirio," I said. "Do you know who Abe Rosenthal is?"

"Of course I know who Abe Rosenthal is—everybody knows who he is," Sirio replied.

I was not about to ask him to give Rosenthal a fond bear hug. I told Sirio that I had called merely to confirm on their reservation. He would take it from there.

I hoped that that little breach of ethics would earn me a silver star from the man who used to think I was a loser. During my time as the restaurant critic I served as the personal reservation service for many masthead editors. At the same time, reporters were forever asking me for dining advice: "My parents are coming to town" or "I'm looking for a romantic place that's not too expensive" or "Where should I eat near Madison Square Garden?" I was happy to help. Although because of the constant interruptions I infrequently wrote in the office. And on the occasions I was in residence, my advice shingle was posted.

The *Times'* publisher, Arthur "Punch" Sulzberger, a wonderful, gentle man, regularly hosted cocktail parties for major advertisers like auto companies and real estate moguls, and brought me along for post-tippling entertainment. Public speaking while depressed is like having your hair ripped out one patch at a time. On these occasions before speaking, I took numerous deep breaths while avoiding all eye contact with the group. Eye contact calls for concentration and a bit of interactivity, which I did not want. A couple of cocktails did not hurt, either. On one occasion I mistakenly looked down to see, a few feet away, Walter Cronkite, smiling. He called me over and asked for a restaurant recommendation for a wedding anniversary.

During that time, Dr. Liebowitz continued to experiment with medications, lots of them. Sometimes we appeared to be approaching long-term improvement, only to see the cycling return. He once informed me with a sigh that my case was "the most complicated I've ever seen." Thanks for sharing that. His official diagnosis was, of all things, "antidepressant induced depression." That's like saying your car has gasoline-provoked stalling. My medication (Nardil), which provided the most relief, could, at certain levels, make me depressed. It was more complicated than that, like everything involving depression. One particularly dreadful evening I feared I would not make it through the night. I asked Dr. Raskin to commit me to a psychiatric hospital. He called Dr. Liebowitz. They agreed that it would not be wise to spend any time in a Manhattan institution of that nature.

"I can do it," said Dr. Liebowitz. "But you won't like it." From the tone of his voice, I knew that it would be hell, so I didn't push it.

At this time, Anne and I were commuting from Westport. Driving home every night after dining out was exhausting. We had to find a residence of some sort in town. It turned out that Pierre knew of a small apartment in his walk-up brownstone on West 55th Street, where he stayed several days a week. It was tiny but adequate, off of Fifth Avenue above a French restaurant called La Bonne Soupe. I liked to boast that we lived around the corner from Tiffany's. The neighborhood was ill-suited for anyone but a childless restaurant critic. There were few amenities like supermarkets, dry cleaners, bodegas, or even a post office. And it was loud—I used to say that we overlooked the Manhattan Academy of Jackhammer Maintenance. But if you wanted to eat out it was a cosmopolitan cornucopia. Our apartment kitchen was so small you practically had to enter sideways, which was no major inconvenience because for ten years we never turned on the stove. In our line of work, eating at home would have been like dozing on guard duty. Moving to the city meant we had to give up our treasured home in Westport. It was a sad day.

Anne and I had been married for five years. I had all but disregarded my past dysfunctional relationships with women before I met her. My "need them/leave them" pathology had been illuminated in therapy, linking it to my father's death and my mother's confounding reaction to it that left the little boy infuriated.

Unfathomably, I began to feel myself drifting away from Anne. She had been at my side since the beginning and remained a calm, steady source of support. We had no marital issues as far as I could ascertain. It wasn't boredom; it was not sex; it wasn't work. It was reminiscent of my calamities with other women in my life, like Helen and Wendy and Jessica and Diane and numerous others. There always came a point at which I became extremely agitated and convinced I had to leave before something very bad transpired. Worse, I always came to believe that my behavior was normal, even ethical.

In a perverse fashion Anne was no longer a participant in my depression, she *was* the depression. Only she knew about my travails; only she had seen the devastation; and she was fearful I would die. I had to get away. I was not thinking about it at the time. I was acting it.

One day at the office I received a call from a French chef named Jean Louie, who owned an eponymous restaurant in Greenwich, Connecticut. I had known him professionally for four or five years, and his virtuosity at the stove had won widespread acclaim. He was going to be in town on Thursday, and would I like to get together for a drink?

I arrived at the rooftop bar at the Novotel in Midtown and found him sitting on a banquette along with a very attractive young woman who worked in his restaurant. Jean Louie appeared to be exerting his amorous charms on the French woman, whose name was Mireille, and he believed that he might score points by introducing her to his famous friend. Mireille had no idea who Bryan Miller was. But we locked eyes and spoke almost exclusively with one another for an hour. I soon abandoned Anne, and we divorced.

Mireille was small in stature and large in intellect, with delicate French features and a high pitched, lilting laugh. She came to the states after her older sister, who was living with an American family in Greenwich, perished in a horrific 1974 discotheque fire in Port Chester, New York, along with twenty-three others, many teenagers. It was in newspapers and on television nationwide. She chose to remain with the family, and became the sous chef at restaurant Jean Louie.

Not only was Mireille alluring, but also, she was unaware of my tormented life, which I considered a major plus. It happened that when I met her I was enjoying a long stretch of well-being, the cause of which being a new drug cocktail conjured up by Dr. Liebowitz. I furtively brought her along on several restaurant reviews and, when I could sneak away from the city, spent time with her in Greenwich. It was despicable behavior, and I knew it, but as with previous women, it seemed perfectly natural. With Mireille, I could imagine that the illness was unreal, a recurring bad dream. As much as Anne became associated with the illness, Mireille embodied emancipation. It was a foolish notion that I would soon pay for. Our secret relationship lasted about six months before it was uncovered, and Anne and I separated.

I had recently purchased a nineteenth century farmhouse in Rhinebeck, New York, about ninety miles up the Hudson River from Manhattan. It was a rambling Victorian-style structure perched on a hill surrounded by century-old elm trees and five grassy acres. Mireille and I loved it there, and it afforded us a respite from our frenetic life in the city. In the first year, we spent a good deal of time renovating the house and exploring the magnificent Hudson Valley. My health declined steadily to the point where I was going to ask for a sabbatical at work.

Mireille, who soon became aware of my depression, decided that we would spend three crazy dining days in the city then retreat to the house where I could try to write. I recall spending an hour and a half on one paragraph—and it was a lousy paragraph. Mireille combined great compassion and heroic fortitude. Every afternoon, when I could no longer function, she would hold my hand and lead me around the village like a blind man.

For part of our marriage, Mireille held a job at a major restaurant developer and consulting firm. At the same time she was studying at the Arts Students League of New York on her way to becoming a professional painter. One of her company's restaurants was called Mama Leone's, a landmark institution for decades that was a huge revenue generator for the company. It had not been reviewed in years so I decided to check it out. It was arguably the worst restaurant I encountered in my dining career. Here are a few nibbles from the review:

Upon being seated you are presented with a platter of Italian breads strewn with cottony cubes of pale tomatoes and garlic, which they call bruschetta, and a rubbery brick of tasteless mozzarella the color of old soap.

As for the main courses, they are scarier than anything conjured up at *Phantom of the Opera* next door. Forget any of the pastas that come with industrial-grade tomato sauce. One mildly satisfying addition to the updated menu is fettuccine with *salsa aurora* (tomato, cream, and porcini). *Fusilli puttanesca* is a bland and soupy mess. Roasted leg of veal with grilled polenta featured two anemic slices of dry meat lying in a puddle of watery juice, along with a pale yellow slab that tastes like day old Cream of Wheat.

I rated it Poor.

Mireille went to the office the following day. No one mentioned the review.

CHAPTER 22
Brain Tumor

IN THE SUMMER OF 1991, while Mireille and I were in Florida with my parents, I experienced an annoying buzz in my right ear. It was sort of an electronic hissing, like an AM radio when you drive through a tunnel, or a rambunctious fly. I did not think much of it until the sound persisted for more than a week. It was truly maddening, and after a short time it demanded all of my attention. A little research indicated that it could have been tinnitus, a condition so debilitating it has provoked suicides. There is no cure. Frequently tinnitus disappears within a couple of months, although it can last for years. Yet another assault on my brain—maybe depression had called in for reinforcements.

Upon returning to New Jersey, I consulted an audiologist in Manhattan. In the examination room was a small glass-enclosed room that held two giant earphones—it reminded me of the privacy booth on a 1950s quiz show. For five minutes I listened to a series of beeps at varying volumes and in alternating ears. The doctor confirmed what I already knew: my hearing was diminished owing to tinnitus. He prescribed antibiotics, and I hissed out the door. The noise greatly diminished within a month. On a follow-up visit, he suggested that I undergo an MRI exam "just to rule out any tumors." Tumors? Let's not go overboard. I did not go.

Ten months later the static reappeared, only someone had turned up the volume. The doctor scolded me for being so casual about a potentially dangerous condition and insisted I undergo the MRI. A week later the results came back. The doctor summoned me into his office. It is never a good sign when a doctor summons you into his office. And if he closes the door, well, good luck.

"Do you see this?" he said, pointing to an x-ray.

"Yes."

"It's a tumor," he revealed reprovingly. "And we have to get it out— sooner than later."

The significance of that bulletin took several seconds to sink in— like whacking your shin on a cocktail table and bracing for the delayed pain.

The doctor explained that it was an acoustic neuroma, which is a growth on the brain that envelopes the auditory nerve, which carries sound from the outside world to the hearing region of the brain. In the year I put off having the MRI, he said, it had grown from the size of a nickle to that of a quarter.

"Acoustic neuromas are usually benign," he added.

"Usually?"

"Almost always benign," he repeated.

At the same time, depression was tightening its screws—I hovered around seven on the mood chart. Add to that headaches, ear aches, and recurrent nosebleeds for no discernible reason. I likened it to rugby—once you are down it doesn't matter how many players pile on top of you. Removal of the tumor would call for severing the nerve, rendering my right ear mere decoration. As it was an ASAP situation, I had to find a surgeon.

There was a pay phone on the corner so I decided to break the news to my mother.

"I have to tell you something," I said, trying to sound casual and upbeat. "I just came from the doctor and it turns out I have a *little* brain tumor—probably benign, no big deal."

After a pause she asked: "It's benign? Do you know this? Did some-one tell you this?"

"Yes, the doctor says it is almost always benign. But I will lose hear-ing in one ear."

"Lose hearing? That's a big deal."

I told her I would call back when I had more information.

I contacted my sister Diane and Mireille, both of whom remained clinically calm.

Though I simply wanted to park at a pub and spend the afternoon with other sympathetic citizens, I returned to the paper and the office of Warren Hoge, a former foreign correspondent who was now an associate managing editor in charge of personnel. I closed the door and explained what had happened. Hoge could not have been more compassionate and supportive. He said that he would tell Rosenthal and Gelb, and we would take it from there. My next call was to Jane Brody, our inexhaustible personal health columnist whose disease of the week column ran for thirty or more years without repetition, as far as I could tell. She was aware of acoustic neuromas and counseled me to be a reporter and interview some experts before choosing a hospi-tal. I contacted three professors at top medical schools. Each recom-mended surgery at the House Ear Clinic, in Los Angeles.

Two weeks later I headed west with Mireille, my mother, and Diane. My surgeon, one Dr. Derald Brackman, was a specialist in acoustic neuromas, and he explained every aspect of the preparation and the operation. He mentioned that an alternative treatment, zapping the tumor with a laser, could save my hearing but there was a possibility the tumor would grow back. And, he cautioned, "We still don't know what shooting lasers into the brain does in the long run." Looking back, I should have taken my chances with the laser. If the tumor returned, we could proceed with surgery. But when you are stressed, you develop a childlike reliance on your doctors, so in effect the choice was already made. (Today laser treatment is considered generally safe, and most acoustic neuromas are treated that way.)

A week before the operation I commenced a battery of testing. A French friend who was in the wine business put his luxurious home at our disposal. As a measure of depression's horror, the surgery itself was number two on my anxiety meter. First was the necessity of ceasing all antidepressant medications for three weeks before the procedure. I had been feeling relatively well at the time, but once the pills were confiscated, I hit the runway without landing gears.

As I was prepping for the big day, Dr. Brackman nonchalantly mentioned that the surgery ran a remote risk of disturbing a facial nerve— the fourth or the sixth nerve as I recall—that has to do with the sense of taste. If it is merely nicked during surgery, the taste buds can be permanently damaged. I took that disclosure with a cool equanimity.

"What!!! *Touch* the nerve??? *Damage taste buds??? Are you joking???*"

"It's very rare," Dr. Brackman said.

"So one slip of the scalpel, and I'm a sports reporter?"

Not to worry, he reassured.

Some years later, Dr. Brackman told me that whenever he gave lectures he talked about the first and only restaurant critic he treated.

"They thought it was funny," he said.

Before surgery I found myself in a lima bean-colored preparation room at Holy Cross Hospital, sitting up on a gurney as an orderly sheared the hair from half of my head. On my legs were extremely tight white stockings, to prevent blood clots during surgery. I was then wheeled into a pale yellow paddock, smaller than the first and smelling of antiseptic.

"How long will I be waiting around in here?" I asked my whistling chauffeur.

"Depends on the doctor," he replied.

A few feet away another client lay on his gurney, head propped up, and sporting a similar haircut.

"What are you in for?" I asked, immediately realizing how moronic it must have sounded.

"Brain tumor," he said, grimly. "You?"

"Same."

From a pair of tinny overhead speakers played a scratchy rendition of Rod Stewart's "Maggie May." Of all my deeply etched memories of that ordeal, the most haunting is that song, which, to this day, can make my palms sweat.

A nurse popped in and pronounced to the nurse, "About fifteen minutes," referring to me.

Another nurse appeared. I said, "I think it's time," referring to a sedative that patients may opt for to calm down before the operation.

Until that point, I had managed to block out images of the procedure. Besides, I was as depressed as hell; this was just another sunny day in California. I had read a bit about it. First they take out the power drill. They plug it in. The skull is about a quarter of an inch thick, so to make a wide incision about three fourths of the way around the ear would take ... I have no idea, depends on the drill size.

I hazily remember entering a brightly lit space and being flopped onto the operating table. There appeared to be a large and inquisitive group of doctors surrounding me. I was told to count to five.

After the procedure, as I was being rolled to the recovery room, Diane came by and began to cry. "You were totally gray—I thought you were dead." There was an explanation for that. To preclude excessive bleeding during brain surgery, the body's metabolism is drastically lowered.

The next thing I knew I was in the intensive care unit, where another nurse was patting my face and shouting, "Wake up! You're finished! Wake up!"

Diane, a nurse, did the same. "It's over! Wake up!" Evidently that was important after brain surgery.

No sooner did things come into focus than the nuclear headache began, which, thankfully, I could ameliorate with a stent attached to a morphine pump. Two hours later I was rolled into my private room, a cheerful spot with a view of downtown Los Angeles. My head was swathed in layers upon layers of white gauze. In half an hour, maybe longer, I was taken to a long corridor and instructed to walk for ten minutes. Two other one-eared zombies, heads down, arms dangling, shuffled ahead of me. I returned to bed.

Shortly thereafter the phone rang. Instinctively, I picked up the receiver with my right hand and held it to my bandaged right ear.

"Bryan?" inquired the caller. "It's Arthur Gelb. Are you all right?"

Flipping the phone to the functioning side, I said yes but that I was a little woozy.

Gelb, notwithstanding all of his responsibilities at the paper, must have made note of the hour of my surgery. We spoke briefly; I closed my eyes imagining what my new life would be like. Half an hour later I received a call from Joseph Giovannini, an architecture writer with whom I shared an office pod. That was all the excitement I could handle that day.

The morning I was discharged, four days later, I was craving victuals that were not served under a plastic lid. I met Jim Sterngold at Chinoise, an excellent Asian restaurant run by star chef Wolfgang Puck. It was heaven—blackened duck, scallion pancakes, grilled seafood. Twenty minutes into the meal I sensed that one half of my face was numb, and drooping. Then I began drooling all over the place. Jim assessed my condition, and we wondered what to do. Nothing, really, aside from using napkins to prevent saliva from dampening the grilled prawns. Before the operation I had been cautioned that some patients experience a "drooping face" that normally resolves itself in two weeks.

Go ahead, pile on top of me.

• • •

Mireille and I married on a resplendent autumn day in 1989, at Rhinebeck's small town hall. The day before the event I needed to drive to Philadelphia for reasons I cannot recall. On the way home the cotton brain syndrome kicked in, and I was so confused and fatigued I had to pull over at a truck stop to nap. I made it home, cursing my plight at such a special time. The wedding day was trying, but I put on a smile, drank Champagne, and soldiered through. I do not think anyone noticed.

My friend Jim Sterngold presented us with the perfect gift—a four-foot tall red maple sapling, which I proudly planted on the sloping front yard. I considered it a metaphor for my new, and rational, life.

Mireille and I loved our life in Rhinebeck. The head bandages had been removed, exposing a deeply etched scar that ran from above the ear down to the earlobe, like a door handle. It attracted a large and appreciative gallery of spectators, both in Rhinebeck and Manhattan. All around were reminders that I had regressed from the symphonic world of stereo to the AM wasteland of mono. One of the more vexing and potentially embarrassing situations is being seated at a large and noisy dinner party or other social function. The guest on my right, the dead ear, is impossible to hear without turning my left ear toward his or her lips. Like other debilitations, I got used to it. Still, I was concerned about heading out on the road without a spare tire. Over time I have compensated to where I can hear stereo music.

But something else came with the package for which I was unprepared. One day in Manhattan I was walking along Eighth Avenue with my friend, Richard. We became separated, and I stopped to allow him to catch up. He called out to me. I heard his voice, however I had no idea where it was coming from. This is called sound localization, the ability to identify from where a sound originates. People can lose it for a number of reasons, most commonly hearing loss in one or both ears. Hearing aids can be helpful for most. For me, they are useless, because the auditory nerve that connects my ear to the brain is severed.

The condition can range from annoying—trying to locate your ringing cell phone—to lethal—not hearing an oncoming bus. On one spring afternoon, I was walking across town to catch a train. I stepped off the curb and was taken down by a honking Ford SUV.

As the days passed, concern for my healing brain was superseded by another question mark. Would the antidepressants that I had so reluctantly terminated before the surgery, and had since resumed, show up for work? Would they still be effective? What if I had to start experimenting again? That could be months. After a week I felt some improvement, which was a relief, but surely it would be short lived. Likely I would resume cycling.

On the subject of cycling, Mireille took advantage of my medical sabbatical to teach me how to ride a motorcycle. I had experienced no balance problems as a result of the surgery, so we felt I could start off slowly—anything to keep me busy. Mireille had learned to ride two years before when, with a girlfriend, she biked to Canada in order to renew her visa. (To do that one must leave the United States and return, with a new stamp in your passport.) We bought two used motorcycles and headed over to the high school parking lot.

I was hooked. The undulating, emerald green Hudson Valley is a paradise for bikers. I pitched a story to my editors at the *Times* called "EZ Diner: A Motorcycle Restaurant Tour of the Hudson Valley." I visited ten spots and rated them on features like driveways (paved good; gravel bad); helmet check (yes, no); and the likelihood of meeting other bikers there (yes, no).

For the next two years, biking was, if not an escape, at least a diversion from my struggles. For whatever reason, I never got around to making my new hobby legal. One day I was pulled over near the center of the village for speeding. The officer demanded the customary paperwork: driver's license (No), insurance card (No), registration (sorry), inspection (nope). At least the officer had a sense of humor. He congratulated me for being the first person he had ever detained who carried absolutely no documents. The bike was placed on a truck and hauled home. I took this as a sign to hang up the helmet.

• • •

About two months after returning to Rhinebeck, and easing back into work, I began to feel myself drifting away from Mireille. There was no palpable reason. Eerily, as with Anne, Mireille gradually metamorphosed from caring spouse and partner into something akin to a nurse, or a sister. One might say that she had taken ownership of the disease, and I had to get away.

Years of therapy had given me a degree of self-awareness that I lacked when I hurt Anne. Still, again I turned selfish and totally unremorseful—and, frankly, crazy. I sought out women who were unaware of my affliction, as if that were a long-term solution. On the day I nudged Mireille out the door I must have carried a wisp of self doubt and regret. My premonitory diary note that day captured it all.

"You really did it this time."

CHAPTER 23
Leaving the Times

IT IS SAID THAT THE tragedy of life is not that man loses, but that he almost wins. In 1993, four years divorced, alone in Rhinebeck, still cycling, and about to lose my apartment, winning was a relative term.

I gave thought to surrendering the restaurant column, the biggest decision in my life. In a just world, I might have remained on the beat. When I announced my move, most people understandably believed that I surrendered out of journalistic indigestion after five thousand meals out, and there was some truth to it. More challenging, actually, was keeping the writing fresh, when well or ill. Reviewing books, theater, art, and cinema allows a writer to draw upon a wide swathe of the human experience. Food writing is more circumscribed. Simply put, how many ways can you describe a roasted chicken? I am exaggerating, of course, but after a decade on the beat I sensed that my shadow was catching up with me. It would be a radical change of lifestyle and stature, and do nothing to mitigate my pain. I would no doubt lose dining "friends" inside and outside of the paper. For years I was a candle that lured countless ingratiating moths. Without the column, I would be a moth.

It was 1993 when I informed Arthur Gelb, and he was most understanding. He tasked me with finding a replacement. One food writer with the experience and ample talent for the job was Ruth Reichl of the *Los Angeles Times*, and she began shortly thereafter.

Progress had been made on the therapy and pharmaceutical fronts, but as my hand-drawn mood chart revealed, not nearly enough. Reading and writing were at times as difficult as they were in 1984, yet somehow I slogged on. But without the column I felt unmoored.

At the *Times*, members of the editorial staff received annual assessments by their supervisors. It seemed rather gratuitous, at least for reporters, because we were assessed every time we turned in a story. But corporations are like that. Up until this point—and I do not know why—I had never been formally evaluated. One day an official looking envelope landed on my desk. The note came from John Montorio, one of my favorite colleagues at the paper, who, at the time, was the deputy Style section editor. We had been good friends for years and he occasionally joined me on reviews. The content of his note—and I recall only the highlights—was that my production had flagged as well as my "enthusiasm and energy." Couldn't argue with that. I was not happy that the brusque assessment came from John—as a friend he could have called me into his office months before for a private consultation. On the other hand, it was his job, like telling the star quarterback that his once laser-sharp passes are now hitting the receiver's crotch. Maybe it was just what I needed. Maybe it was time to go.

Joe Lelyveld, the brilliant and amiable executive editor, was in his office that afternoon, so I skulked in unannounced. He was attentive as I unfurled my story and told him I could no longer remain at the paper. He was very sympathetic, although it was evident that he was at a loss as to what to say. He offered to assign me to a less taxing post until I felt better, perhaps on the copy desk. I demurred. Besides, the copy desk at the *Times* is anything but relaxing; it is a grueling and thankless existence, like an oarsman on a Phoenician galley. Besides, what would people think? Bryan Miller on the copy desk? By that point, I had little expectation that the illness would relent anytime soon, barring a Salk-like pharmaceutical breakthrough. I thanked Joe and said I really had to resign but would keep in touch, which, of course, I never did. Perhaps if there were someone in life, like a wife, to discuss my thoughts in a rational, big picture way, things would have worked out differently. At that moment, however, I just wanted to get the hell out of the building.

I returned to my desk—a landfill of newspapers, culinary magazines, restaurant menus, reference books, coffee cups, and notes for a story in progress. My inglorious departure included a quick visit with my good friend Mort Stone, a photo editor, not to confess what I was up to but to plan a dinner. I would fill him in then. There was a visit to the pressroom; I would miss those guys. I slipped out via the truck bay onto West 43rd Street, never to hold a warm newspaper again.

CHAPTER 24
The Lost Year

THE MAGNITUDE OF MY ACTIONS that day was not immediate. The first impression was relief, although what kind of relief comes with walking out on your career, forgoing a salary, facing eviction from your apartment, entering seclusion in the country, and still being depressed, I don't know. I walked up to a fine Irish pub on West 57th Street called Kennedy's, a hangout of mine only five blocks from my apartment. It was all brass and gleaming wood and nonstop blarney, with a large dining room in the back anchored by a large working fireplace. The Irish fare was adequate and authentic. It seemed like a fitting foxhole where I could hide out and have a serious conversation with myself about the future.

"Hey young fella," snapped a jaunty Irish gentleman, Ryan O'Shea by name. I had spent many evenings at the pub with him watching soccer matches and talking politics. He was a colorful story teller and possessed a capacious memory for jokes. I do not believe there was ever a time when he was not carrying a new one in his pocket. I always forgot jokes as soon as I heard them, but this was a landmark occasion, and it stuck with me.

"Bryan, have you heard the one about the preachers and the house of ill repute?"

"Try me."

"Well, you have Paddy and Kevin sitting in a pub that was right across from a house of ill repute. They spot a protestant minister walking down the street. He stops at the house, knocks on the door, and is let in. Paddy says: 'Oh, mother of Mary, look at that—a man of the cloth frequenting a place like that. Shameful!' A few minutes later a rabbi approaches. He knocks on the door and is ushered in. Kevin says: 'Do you see that? What a hypocrite, what a betrayal of his flock!' Shortly after, a Catholic priest arrives. He knocks on the door, and is let in. Says Paddy:

'Ah, what a shame. One of the girls must have died.'"

It was my first laugh in weeks.

"You're here on the early side," Ryan observed.

"I quit my job."

"Nooo! You quit your job, the best job in the world!"

"I'm afraid I did."

"Son. Get your wits about you! Jesus, Mary, and Joseph, what could have driven you to this decision?"

"Long story. Another time."

"It better be a good one."

"Oh, it's a good one all right."

Much of the following year is a blank slate. I had some sort of job at an online city guide. What I did, don't ask. Nor with whom I worked. Of my personal life, little remains. Clearly, I functioned on some level, if only to pay the mortgage, but I have no recollections. It was like drifting out of a coma. My guess is that the brain can tolerate only so much tension before parts of the hard drive crash.

My depression cycling was uneven, sometimes two to three weeks up and the same span down. After a couple of months of that, I discovered something shocking: my crashes appeared to be linked to Anne and Mireille. It sounds crazy, but any mention of them, photos of them, even memories of them, pushed me off the cliff. They were Marley's ghost. It was like having two depressions. The triggers could be as trivial as seeing a necktie received as a gift, a photo, or a poignant memory. It was so enraging that I tossed out all kinds of marriage-related merchandise: furniture, kitchenware, coats, lamps, quilts, and books. Dr. Raskin called them "triggers." It became so noxious that, when in the city, I had to walk with my head down to avoid them. Every time I parked in my driveway I could not avoid something that was a potential super trigger: The red maple tree Jim Sterngold gave Mireille and me on our wedding day. I attempted to ignore the innocent little houseguest tree for a while, but it taunted me. At 2:00 a.m. on a wind-swept winter night, I arose, descended to the cellar, and seized an axe. Under the ghostly silhouette of a nearly full moon, I chopped it down and dragged it into the woods.

At that time my mother, divorced from Ben and alone, was living in her condo on the ocean north of Palm Beach, Florida. Looking for something to occupy her time, she acquired a real estate license. Her personality was ideal for that line of work although her heart was not in it. And, in her late fifties, she was not ready for bingo. Then God came forth in a mysterious way.

One day she was walking along the beach and noticed a familiar face coming in her direction.

"Lou!" she exclaimed.

Lucian Fletcher Jr. was a cardiologist at Newton Memorial Hospital, where she had worked for ten years. His wife had died from brain cancer some years before. He, too, owned a condo on that beach. After a six month tropical courtship, they married and moved to his stone farmhouse in Fredon, outside of Newton. Lucian was a perfect match for Dorothy: handsome, intellectual, fun loving, and generous. They reunited with their local friends; they travelled the world and entertained and flew in his vintage Cessna up and down the East Coast. At home they loved to put on Kenny Rogers and slow dance in the living room.

Lucian was a renowned figure in Sussex County, one of the last physicians to make house calls, often to farmhouses in remote areas in the middle of the night. Some patients paid him with vegetables, pickled foods, or moonshine. He told me that in thirty years he almost never slept the night through. We were big football fans, and every fall we drove or flew down to his alma mater, Princeton University, for sumptuous tailgate parties. For a *Times'* feature we flew to Nova Scotia in search of original Cajun food, and to Massachusetts on a five-restaurant-three-day marathon. One could not have had a better step-father. Lucian had four children all within an hour away but, curiously, they pretty much ignored him outside of major holidays. Over the years he saved my life, literally, several times. I was forever grateful and tried at every turn to make up for it.

They were perfect on so many levels, including food. My mother was a capable cook. She specialized in leftovers. If there was the tiniest sliver of meatloaf remaining, or a pinky sized morsel of chicken breast, they were wrapped in aluminum foil and arrayed throughout the refrigerator for an indeterminate length. Much to my mother's con-sternation, I never ate anything from that refrigerator. Lucian, having subsisted on dreary hospital food for most of his life, uncritically con-sumed whatever artifact my mother placed in front of him, and loved it. I was so pleased to see my mother finally happy.

CHAPTER 25
ECT

THE SMALL WAITING ROOM WAS the color of French dressing, made more dispiriting by a gallery of Walmart style art on the walls and uncomfortable plastic chairs. We were fifteen minutes early. The only other patient was a young woman, maybe forty, wearing oversized sunglasses and a headscarf, accompanied by a slight, fidgety man, most likely her husband. They held hands tightly. She was definitely not in a chatty mood as she studied a pamphlet entitled "ECT—What You Should Know."

By that time I knew more than I cared to, so I picked up an outdated copy of *Sports Illustrated*. Soon there arrived a tall, cadaverous man with croissant-shaped crescents under his eyes. He must have overslept, for one side of his pillow-matted hair was swept up in a defiant wave. A few minutes later entered two more customers: an attractive middle aged lady in a beige turtleneck sweater, followed by an expressionless fifty-ish fellow wearing an ill-fitting sports jacket and the resigned expression of someone whose second tee shot had landed in the drink. He placed a briefcase under the chair.

"You don't think this guy is going to work after the treatment, do you?" I whispered to Lucian.

"Could be," he replied. "But you are not allowed to drive."

Lucian, a spirited eighty-one, had awoken me at 4:00 a.m. for the snowy two hour drive to Princeton Hospital. I suppose I should have been nervous, but after a decade of repeated suffering and disappointment, it was just another trip to the store.

ECT—electroconvulsive therapy—is usually doled out in a series of six to ten weekly sessions, so it was likely that some of those in the room were old hands. I studied their faces, scanning for signs of optimism or improvement, but little was in evidence.

Approaching my fifties, and five years departed from the *Times*, I was fairly desperate after six months of moping around my parents' house, with no indication that the haze would dissipate anytime soon—or ever. Even so, I had never given much thought to ECT. Shock treatment, I had presumed, was for those at the polar extremes, severe mania or nearly catatonic depression. I had not reached the latter, but my compass was pointing in that direction.

ECT was Lucian's idea. He had firsthand knowledge of its mysterious ways, first as a medical resident in the late 1940s, and later involving his father. Lucian Fletcher Sr. owned a lakeside resort hotel in Branchville, New Jersey, from the late 1940s through the mid-1960s. He was a personable if not outgoing man, in overall good health, but for many years stoically grappled with his depression.

"Every once in a while," Lucian told me, "he would get very quiet and retreat to his room—sometimes for a week." Despite experiments with the tentative medications of the day, he gradually worsened to the point that one morning, as Lucian was driving him to the grocery store, he flung open the car door and bailed out. Luckily, they were just putting along.

Antidepressant medications were in a nascent stage; in fact, until the mid-1950s, some physicians continued to administer addictive opiates as a short-term balm for "extreme melancholy," a term that goes back to the Middle Ages. Amphetamines were prescribed as well, to little lasting effect. The introduction of tricyclic antidepressants in 1958 revolutionized psychopharmacology. These boosted the brain's supply of norepinephrine and serotonin, chemicals that tend to be deficient in clinically depressed patients.

Then there was the lobotomy, a surgical Hail Mary pass devised by a Portuguese neurologist in 1935. Severing nerve fibers that connected the frontal lobes, it was believed by some, could calm extremely agitated patients and ameliorate some other mood disorders. It could also leave one with the emotional vitality of a kumquat. Its efficacy was uncertain at best. Almost from the beginning, the American Medical Association opposed the practice as too dangerous. Bill Bryson described it in his book *The Body*. The Babe Ruth of what was called a "frontal lobotomy" was a controversial physician named Walter Jackson Freeman, who believed it could straighten out individuals with a range of maladies, from drunkenness to homosexuality. He once performed 225 procedures in twelve days. His brisk but gruesome technique involved taking a household ice pick into the brain, entering through the eye socket, breaking through the skull with a hammer, and wiggling around the tool to sever neural connection. About two-thirds of Freeman's patients saw no improvement. Joseph P. Kennedy, father of the future president, had a twenty-three-year-old daughter, Rosemary. She was a dreamy, quiet, and sometimes detached young woman, but not mentally ill by prevailing definitions. Her father believed a lobotomy could well be effective. She received the icepick treatment, to no avail, and passed the remaining sixty-three years in institutions.

Lobotomies fell out of use as medications became more sophisticated and their success rate surged to more than 70 percent—still lower than ECT, supposedly about 90 percent. Then again, what does "success" mean? Is providing relief for a month, or six months, a success? By that metric, I was cured more than seventy times.

Lucian drove his father down to Columbia Presbyterian Hospital, in Manhattan (his medical school alma mater). ECT treatments in the 1950s were far more aggressive than those I experienced. It was administered without muscle relaxants, so when the switch was flipped, inducing a grand mal seizure, the patient might flail about. Grand mal seizures, or generalized tonic-clonic seizures, are seizures that involve muscle contractions, muscle rigidity, and loss of consciousness. They result from abnormal electrical activity in the brain, either naturally or induced as in ECT. For that reason they were strapped down.

ECT progressed considerably in the ensuing years and became widely accepted by the public as a beneficial and humane mode of treatment. But not for long. In 1975 came the movie *One Flew Over the Cuckoo's Nest*, which portrayed ECT as the most malevolent form of torture since the medieval rack. The vastly exaggerated portrait had Jack Nicholson secured to a gurney, thrashing uncontrollably while zapped with enough electricity to illuminate Hartford. In terms of PR, that scene set ECT back more than twenty years. Even today, some people believe the cinematic portrait to be accurate.

Such is the inscrutability of the human brain after more than a century of scientific inquiry that the precise underpinnings of clinical depression remain elusive. No wonder, really, for the complex four pound mass of squishy Jell-O between our ears is infinitely more powerful and complex than anything yet discovered in the universe. In Bill Bryson's informative and entertaining book, *The Body*, we learn just how powerful. For example, sitting quietly, doing nothing at all, he explains, your brain churns through more information in thirty seconds than the Hubble Space Telescope has processed in thirty years. A morsel of cortex about the size of a grain of sand can hold two thousand terabytes of information, enough to store all of the movies ever made, or about 1.2 billion copies of his book.

We can watch colorful neurons dart about on a computer screen; we can mess with your circuit board using drugs. We know where memories are stored but not what they are. And why, in depression, do neurons suddenly turn on us like schoolyard hoodlums, then suddenly cease and go home?

As of yet, no biological markers for depression have been identified, so we cannot predict one's likelihood of contracting the disease. It is estimated that up to 40 percent of those suffering from depression carry a genetic link, which explains why that is the first question posed by mental health professionals.

Lucian's dad underwent his first dose of ECT without incident and returned to his son in the waiting room.

"I couldn't believe it!" Lucian recalled. "He was a different person, his old self! He never felt depression again."

Into our waiting room arrived a nurse who, judging by her chirpy demeanor, was having a very good day. Through the crack in the door I spotted a long room with four beds separated by white curtains. She beckoned three patients. A minute later another nurse appeared. She, too, seemed to be having a good day, or perhaps it was part of the job description.

"Bryan?"

I turned to Lucian and, in a lame attempt at gallows humor, said: "If I don't recognize you when I come out, take me to the diner for breakfast anyway."

I was escorted to one of the beds in the center of the room and left to idle for what seemed like three days but was probably only fifteen minutes. The nurse came in and handed me a white hospital gown. This would be the first of ten biweekly treatments.

"You just relax now. Dr. Khoury will be along shortly," she said.

Relax?

I was not terribly anxious. After all, I had but two cards left to play: ECT or DOA. I examined something on a side table that resembled a car battery with colored wires dangling from it. A low humming sound came from a nearby bed. I became anxious.

Dr. Khoury appeared, wearing a long white coat and the subdued expression of someone who could do the procedure in his sleep.

"Good morning, Bryan," he said in a vaguely Middle Eastern accent. Slight, gentle, soft-spoken, and professorial, he appeared to be in his mid-fifties. I could not help but notice his hands—soft, smooth, and with long thin fingers. In my research I learned that Dr. Khoury was widely considered the Yo Yo Ma of the electro

shock set. We had met twice before, so he dispensed with the badinage and moved to the task at hand. Next to him was an intense
looking medical intern who studied his every move, as well as an
anesthesiologist.

"Do you mind if Dr. Jones watches the procedure?" Dr. Khoury
asked.

At that point, I didn't care if the Rockettes stopped by for a look
see. I just wanted it over. Under the supervision of Dr. Khoury, the
intern was allowed to fiddle with a wire connected to the car battery,
and he must have been new at it, judging from the time required to
accomplish the task.

In our previous meeting, Dr. Khoury had explained what to expect.
"I must tell you that you may experience some memory loss afterwards," he'd cautioned. "But it will return—it always returns." I could
deal with that.

He would explain again how ECT worked—or at least how he
thought it worked. To this day, no one can say for sure why passing
an electrical current through the brain can alleviate depression and
certain other forms of mental illnesses.

In the previous month I had read a fair amount on the subject. The
best image I can come up with is a pool table holding a rack of colored
balls. A player rears back and blasts them in all directions. Somehow,
it disrupts the faulty synaptic connections that may be causing mis-
chief, while at the same time releasing serotonin and chemicals that
might be lacking.

"Mr. Miller, I am going to put you into a mild sleep," said the anesthesiologist, inserting a stent into my left arm. I soon became extremely
dizzy, as if I were swirling down a drain, and then lights out. The next
thing I recalled was Dr. Khoury standing over me.

"How do you feel?" he asked.

"Okay, I guess. It's over already?"

That was it? I almost felt as if I did not get my money's worth. I
was a bit disoriented, the way you feel upon awakening from a crazy

dream, but otherwise fine. In five minutes I was dressed. I thanked the nurse for a great time and returned to the waiting room.

"How do you feel?" Lucian asked.

"Hungry. Can we go to the diner?"

I could not determine if I was still depressed. Presumably, ECT was particularly susceptible to the placebo effect; that's a hell of a placebo.

In the ensuing weeks the Star Diner, three miles north of Princeton Hospital, came to serve as my unofficial recovery room. We would settle into one of the big red booths, order weak coffee and breakfast, and commence a debriefing and memory session:

"Do you remember driving down here this morning?"

"Yes."

"What was the last football game we went to?"

"Princeton-Yale."

"What color is your car?"

"Red."

That sort of thing. I always had French toast.

Unlike Lucian's dad, I did not enjoy sudden emancipation with the first treatment—nor the second, nor the sixth. Dr. Khoury suggested we wait several weeks and, if need be, go into extra innings: six more. He attempted to alleviate my disappointment and fear by pointing out that some patients do not improve until several weeks after the final treatment. I did not believe him, of course, and began to fear that even that ordeal would come to nothing. Then what?

Things took a turn for the worse. About a week after session number twelve, still living with my parents, I began to sense my memory was evaporating like water on a scorching saucepan. I could not recall what I had done the previous week. I vaguely remembered attending a group therapy meeting some weeks before but had no idea who was there nor what was discussed.

"Dr. Khoury told you to expect this," Lucian asserted.

Yes, a little amnesia around the edges for a while would be tolerable.

But when it actually settles in, all bets are off. I feared I would live out my days in the present tense.

As my condition worsened and the anxiety mounted, restrictions were placed on my movements. Driving was out. My parents feared if I attempted to drive to town I might wind up in Delaware. Increasingly agitated, I repeatedly paced around the kitchen island, babbling about nothing. Lucian called in a prescription for Xanax.

Dr. Khoury, expressing exasperation at the ineffectiveness of the treatment, decided to put on a crowd-pleasing double header—ten more consecutive sessions.

"This should help," he said.

One might fantasize that living without memory could be liberating. If you cannot recall further back than breakfast, then any misdeeds before then are wiped clean. Like Catholic confession. If only that were the case. In a word, it is terrifying.

Partway into the treatments my mother and I decided to drive up to my farmhouse in Rhinebeck, some two hours away, to check on the premises and retrieve some spring clothing. I insisted upon taking the wheel. Everything went fairly well for about thirty miles as we drove through the rolling farm country of northern New Jersey. We soon reached a hamlet where the road ended, requiring us to go left or right. I had passed through this ramshackle town a hundred times, but today had no clue what to do. Straight ahead was a dilapidated general store that appeared vaguely familiar. Aside from that, it could have been Philadelphia.

Not wishing to alarm my mother, I rolled the dice and turned left. Before long, even my feeble brain suspected we were headed in the wrong direction. I pulled off the road and lay my head on the steering wheel, nearly weeping.

"I don't know where to go," I whimpered.

At that moment, my mother—who had gamely endured my zombie-like company for six months—fell apart.

"I don't think I can take this anymore," she sobbed, pulling a tissue from her purse. "I want to go home."

"We can't go home—besides, I have to check on the house."

There we sat, on a dank, gray morning in some godforsaken settlement in upstate New York, my mother weeping while I stared incomprehensibly at a map.

She regained her composure. "I'll drive," she sniffled. "Hand me the map."

Miraculously, we arrived at the house before noon, where we were greeted by George Warner, my longtime caretaker. In his mid-seventies, George looked sixty, and could easily work alongside fifty-year-olds. Thick and broad-shouldered, set low to the ground for better traction, he possessed a sunny disposition and a fine gray goatee.

George kept the wheels spinning at my farmhouse, a life saver for someone who is congenitally inept when it comes to chores involving hammers and power drills. And there was plenty to do in my cherished six-bedroom, hundred-year-old farmhouse.

In the years following my abrupt departure from the *Times*, I lived alone in Rhinebeck. George stopped by nearly every day, even when there were no home improvements on the agenda. When depressed, I welcomed his undemanding conversation.

Then too, I think he just wanted to get out of his own claustrophobic house. His miniature blue cabin with a small barn out back enjoyed a lovely view of the Dutchess County countryside. His wife, Bunny, whom I rarely saw outside, entered my home only once in eleven years—for a holiday champagne toast, and that was after I drove to her house and practically dragged her out. She possessed a doll collection that had literally taken over their home. Every square inch, upstairs and down, was infested with antique dolls: frilly dolls, dancing dolls, baby dolls, scary dolls, *Gone with the Wind* dolls, Chinese dolls. They occupied the stairway, the kitchen, and stood guard in the bathroom. Sitting in the living room, I felt as if hundreds of tiny glass eyes were staring at me—it was beyond creepy. No wonder George preferred hanging around with a depressed guy.

Following a quick lunch in the historic little village, we drove—my mother at the wheel—back to Newton. I knew she was at wit's end.

"We have to come up with a plan," she announced in the car.

"Great," I said.

"You know we are always here for you, and I love you."

"Me, too."

"Why do you never say I love you? Never."

"I don't know."

"I wonder about it."

"I don't know, maybe I don't say that to anybody."

"Everybody needs assurances. We are all afraid of something. Like someday being alone."

"OK, let's make that new plan tomorrow."

In Newton, my anxiety escalated over the next few days. One morning I alarmed my sister, Diane, when I again began circling the kitchen island, cursing and muttering about losing control for good.

Lucian called Dr. Khoury, who prescribed the anti-anxiety drug Ambien. Within fifteen minutes of taking the drug, I was calm—depressed as hell, but calm. Dr. Khoury asked us to come down to Princeton.

By the time we arrived, my agitation was such, I am told, that I began thumping my head against the wall. Dr. Khoury slipped me some pills and remanded me to a "unit." The unit resembled a recess space for first graders: circular and partly glassed in, it featured a giant TV, numerous board games, a ping-pong table, a card table, and a couple of wrinkled magazines. The majority of the residents were between twenty and thirty years of age, and appeared harmless.

Trapped, I claimed a seat near the TV but did not watch it. Soon, a nurse holding a tray handed out some sort of punch, which I declined (I had seen too many spy movies to fall for that). A large middle-aged man with a suet complexion and broken eyeglasses ambled over to me.

"Hey," I snarled, "Where the hell am I?"

"This is for patients who need to calm down," he said. "At least that's what they told me. The calm down tank."

"Great. Are you calm? How long you been in?"

"Two days. They tell you when you are calm."

We were asked to attend a group-therapy meeting, which I found excruciatingly silly so I left. I do not recollect dinner, or where I slept—or if I slept at all. At daybreak, Dr. Khoury appeared with my parents.

"Get me out of here!" I barked through the glass. The doctor entered the room and checked my pulse. We spoke for a while about my mood and anxiety level, and then I was liberated under parental care.

Before long—maybe six weeks after the final ECT session—the missing pages of my memory started reappearing. Just like that. However my elation was tempered by the realization that two months of aggressive ECT had been fruitless. Dr. Khoury again tried to put a positive spin on things by noting that sometimes the effects of ECT are not seen for a number of months. Sure. He confided to my parents that it was extremely rare to have a patient not respond at all.

Back in Newton, where the highlight of my week was a haircut and lunch at the Andover Diner, I noticed in the local newspaper, a small ad concerning a depression discussion group that convened on Tuesday evenings at a former Abbey a couple of miles out of town. It was a spooky place, thick granite and slate, with sharp turrets in silhouette against a brilliant winter moon. I entered a large, high ceilinged room supported by massive timber beams and with a simple wooden cross over the entrance. As I looked around it appeared that the space was performing double duty: holy sanctum and storage unit. Everywhere there were retired wooden pews, folding chairs, and boxes. About eight individuals of varying ages sat in a semi-circle. I had no inkling that it would be one of the most profound experiences of my life.

As I have noted, depressed people infrequently talk with normal people about their travails. They talk at people, because no one who has not gone through their torment is at all capable of understanding. Here I did not need to utter a word nor shake a hand. It was all in the eyes—the anguish, the loneliness, the spiritual fatigue, the yearning to survive. I felt what they were feeling; it was as if they could see through me. I was home.

A soft-spoken woman who served as the moderator perused the room. I was asked to introduce myself. She inquired if anyone had updates from last week. A woman named Jenny, I think, thin and frail, wearing oversized eyeglasses, volunteered that she continued to have difficulties performing her duties in the office and feared that one of her superiors might catch on. Immediately, three others raised their hands. I wanted to raise my hand, too, but held back for the moment. For about five minutes the participants suggested strategies—real strategies, not just hugs and encouragement.

One participant said she should try working in intense spurts, with short breaks in between: "It's like removing a pot of boiling water from the burner—the bubbles will stop and afford you a little time to regroup. And you can look forward to the next break."

Another woman raised her hand.

"This may sound silly," she allowed, "but I have a bunch of little techniques to use when needed." She read from a sheet of paper. "Do not feel obligated to socialize; give yourself a break once in a while. You deserve it. Do some work at home if possible to lighten the load when you are at work. Do not confide in someone for the sake of confiding—it should be a person who really cares for you and might be helpful. Stay on top of your medications. Do not miss doses. If they are not working after six months, consider finding another psychopharmacologist. Talk therapy may seem terribly slow and frustrating at times, but keep at it. Good things could be happening that you are not aware of."

Some participants described difficulties with medications and inquired about others taking similar drugs; several struggled with family challenges. It was not so much the advice that lifted my spirits, although that was beneficial, but rather the honesty and sense of community the gathering offered. In the second meeting another moderator, a short, fleshy young man wearing a sports jacket, raised a question that caught the audience—and me—off guard. After relating his heart-rending bouts with depression that left him divorced, under-employed, and living in a small apartment a quarter the size of his previous residence, he asked the gathering in a solemn tone:

"Is happiness a birthright?"

No one was prepared for that one. A long silence.

"Yes, I think," affirmed a middle-aged woman wearing a colorful sixties style dress. "It's like good health—you are born with it, you deserve it, but it can be easily taken away if you do not remain strong."

A young man in a New York Giants hoodie chimed in: "It has to be, otherwise what's the point of being human? We can't be placed here to suffer."

"Good observations," the moderator intoned. "Let's think about it and follow up next week."

At the end of the meeting I went up and asked the moderator who he was. Turns out he was a religious man of sorts, not a priest, not a formal pastor, not a rabbi, but a trained counselor who dropped in on patients at Newton Memorial Hospital.

I attended several more uplifting meetings before they were suspended for the remainder of winter.

My mother urgently needed a break from my needy presence and arranged for me to spend time with my sister, Diane, in Hillsborough, New Jersey, ten miles north of Princeton. Her husband, Joe, is a doctor, so I suppose it was a prudent move.

CHAPTER 26
Checking Out

I REMAINED WITH DIANE AND Joe for five muddled months. Fortunately, I had some freelance copy editing to distract me, gathering unpublished Pierre Franey recipes for a new book. I exercised, tried to read, played with their cats, and watched TV. I told my mother and Lucian not to visit. They had endured enough.

Back in Rhinebeck I was still broke, alone, and without any semblance of a life strategy. One day a bank statement arrived in the mail and pronounced that my net worth was $16.10. I laughed, and taped it to the wall.

The little apartment in Midtown was no longer affordable. To cover the previous three months' rent I sold a beautiful pine armoire, an early American table, a two thousand dollar guitar, and two Oriental rugs. Freelance editing was bringing in a dribble of income, and I had some book royalties, but on that memorable day it was either food or gas. I bought a turkey thigh, six red potatoes, a baguette, and seven dollars worth of gas.

Fulltime employment was largely out of the picture. There was a position at the Culinary Institute of America, in Hyde Park, New York, teaching writing four times a year in the bachelor of arts program. I was a longtime friend of the school president, Tim Ryan, and was acquainted with some of the faculty. I was a familiar face on campus and had spoken at a number of graduations. How difficult could teaching be?

In preparation I assembled packages of reading material and writing exercises. I awoke the morning of the first class seriously fogged in. Of all days. It was too late to postpone the lesson. I boosted my medications, but all that did was leave me trembling badly. My mouth was as dry as sandpaper. About twenty exceedingly young students were in attendance, all in chefs' whites. I asked one to fetch me some water. My lesson plan for the first session called for writing on the blackboard. I dropped the chalk, twice. There was no way I could write, and my mouth was so dry I spoke at a near whisper. The dean of the bachelors' program arrived and took a seat in the back of the room. I began blathering on about writing, incoherently I am sure, and passed around sheets of paper for them to write three paragraphs about themselves. I glanced at the clock—class was scheduled for two hours. We had barely used forty minutes. Class dismissed.

My performance at the second class was hardly better—I had taken a large dose of tranquilizers to tamp down the shakes. These lulled me into a trancelike state. The dean dropped in again, expecting the worst. I did not disappoint. After another pitiful spectacle—I sensed that the students also had doubts about their famous instructor—the dean called me into his office.

"So, how do you think you're doing?" he asked.

"Between bad and dismal."

I wanted to say that if we scheduled classes around my manic depression cycles things would take a turn for the better. He suggested I improve my meager pedagogical skills at another institution.

Clearly, I did not have the mental clarity for cerebral enterprises. My friend Stew Leonard, whose family owns a group of popular food stores, took me on to analyze store recipes, which were written for commercial quantities, and translate them for home use. That should have been a breeze; I had written recipes for years. At that time I was healthy for about eight days at a time followed by eight days down. The job proved too much—it called for much painful interaction with staff members—and I had to leave. I tried my hand at book editing, but at times I had to read the same page three times to understand it, and my pace was glacial. I was fired.

During that time Dr. Liebowitz kept me alive by juggling medications, although too often they "almost" succeeded—a three foot leap over a five foot ditch. Numerous times, when I was at wits ends, I left a message at his office. He always called back, usually in late evening, and talked me down. There might be an adjustment of the medication.

I had been making measurable progress on the therapy front with Dr. Raskin. He had doubled down on my relationship with my mother upon my father's death, and how it was the nexus of my problems with all women.

At times I saw Dr. Raskin twice in one day even though I could not afford it—although he was kind enough to offer many discounts (At times Dr. Liebowitz did not charge me at all). One early spring day I was close to being committed; Dr. Raskin sensed the depth of my despair and called me at home one evening, but I was too distressed to answer. I just sat there staring at the hearth. A short time later there was shouting and pounding on the door. It was the police, responding to Dr. Raskin's request that they check on me. That perked me up; I told them I was fine.

The party rolled on: On a fall morning I left the house before sunrise to drive to Hartford regarding an editing gig. Walking down the front steps, in complete darkness, I mistakenly turned right instead of left and plummeted ten-feet-down onto a cement driveway. I lay there in immense pain. Shouts for help went unheard for five minutes— there were no close neighbors and infrequent cars. Eventually two young men from far down the road hustled up the driveway, assessed my condition, and summoned an ambulance. I was examined at the hospital and told it was nothing serious, just take these crutches, and I would feel better in a couple of weeks. When I described the incident to Lucian, he was skeptical of the diagnosis and drove me down to his hospital in Newton. It came out that it was a cracked pelvis. That was better than breaking a hip, he said, if that was any consolation.

Lying on a couch while unable to walk, with no place to walk anyway because I had no money, confined to a half furnished living room, depressed, lonely, and fearing that soon a strange family would be cooking in my kitchen—that can summon some very dark thoughts indeed.

Having a good deal of *quality time in my household,* and with my eyes glazed over from watching Turner Classic Movies, I turned to a task that had been avoided for decades because, well, it could bring bad luck—hah. Plan my memorial service. It was presumptuous, of course, as many personal friends had been thrust out the door as I became increasingly withdrawn, and most professional acquaintances, some of whom for years were lavishly nourished as restaurant reviewing guests, saw little point in staying in touch.

Be that as it may, a little scripting might help whoever is stuck with the assignment of hosting it. I often thought it would be funny if, after the customary eulogies, the decedent said a few words. Why not? There will hardly be anyone there.

Four people would be asked to make remarks.

Tim Zagat, longtime friend and colleague.

Jim Sterngold, a dear friend going back to our days at the *Times.*

Benson Ginsburg, my oldest friend, from the early 1970s.

Glenn Dopf, another longtime friend and dining team regular.

Remarks from Bryan Miller:

Hello everyone. Thank you for coming. This may seem a little spooky for you— imagine what it is like for me. I had a rough ride but I suppose it was better than no ride at all. Many of you were kind and patient, putting up with my occasional instability and vanishing acts. Depression is a hideous and mysterious affliction. It comes and goes as it pleases, and always overstays its welcome. If you are aware of someone who is struggling, be kind but not patronizing, and get them into treatment.

I had to run ... but take care, stay safe, and help those less fortunate than you ... and say nice things about me once in a while—or else I will return at night and move around your furniture.

As I have said—and it is just my observation—many, if not most, depressed people who attempt suicide do not reach that state as a result of a thoughtful assessment of their situations and weighing of the options. It is largely impulsive. They just want to end the pain. That's all. My mansion of woes had many rooms, compounded by the realization that there was no "cure" for depression, and that likely there would not be one in my lifetime, nor maybe that of my son Sean.

Snow fell hard on a Wednesday evening in January. I resolved to put an end to the travesty in a decisive, dignified manner. It would not only end the pain but also lift a tremendous burden from my mother and Lucian and Diane. It has been said that suicide does not end the suffering, it only passes it on. True, but I had already afflicted my family with ten years of heartbreak. I suppose suicide is the ultimate selfish act. I tried not to think about how they would take the news. It would not be a complete surprise; they must have spoken of the possibility. Death was no stranger to Lucian. He would take care of everything by entering doctor mode. My mother ... I was not so sure. She had an uncommon capacity to rally in times of great adversity. When my heart was running out the clock the doctors were very agitated and noisy. My mother stood there, calmly, as if I were getting a flu shot.

"It was your heart," she told me afterward. "Lucian can take care of that."

Same with the brain tumor. She took control, along with Diane.

It must have crossed my parents' minds that the depression could ultimately take me down. Having seen me at my worst, they might be sympathetic to my actions. I decided there would be no final note. It would probably make things worse. In her excellent book on suicide, *Night Falls Fast*, Kay Redfield Jamison wrote:

"Each way to suicide is its own: intensely private, unknowable, and terrible. Suicide will have seemed to its perpetrator the last and best of bad possibilities, and any attempt by the living to chart this final terrain of a life can be only a sketch, maddeningly incomplete."

My destination was the Beekman Arms and Delamater Inn, circa 1776, the cultural and touristic anchor of the village. I pulled open the massive oak door and approached the two hundred-year-old stone hearth. In the back of the inn is a dark old wood-lined tavern with a handsome bar that on weekdays is frequented mostly by townsfolk. I had passed many happy evenings there with Mireille, and alone—it is a difficult place to leave. Because of the weather there were few patrons, which was just as well.

I settled in at the corner of the bar, far enough from two other patrons to discourage conversation.

"Roads plowed yet?" a man inquired.

"No," I replied. "Roads aren't plowed yet."

"Maybe we'll have to spend the night here."

"Wouldn't be the worst place."

I reached into my shirt pocket and found a prescription for one of my antidepressants. Was it some kind of sign? A little late for that. I had come to accept that the pills had, in the end, failed to stop the cycling. And it was possible that I would wear out the cushion of psychotherapy as well.

The first two old fashioneds performed what they were hired to do—nudge me further in the direction of indifference. There were no profound thoughts, no regrets, no ontological musings, no poetry. Those stages were behind me. I recalled my depression help group in Newton where we were asked: do you fear death? Upbeat topic. Not really, I replied, I have been there so many times I know where to find street parking.

Franz Kafka posited that the meaning of life is that it ends; that is, virtually everything we undertake during our long weekend on the planet is provoked by the grudging awareness of our expiration. What will our legacy be? Children? Professional accomplishments? Building a home? Teaching others? Kindness? What do I have of any consequence? I would like to say kindness, but that is for Anne and Mireille to judge.

Drink three (They made stingy, though potent, cocktails) was enjoyed slowly. I was not drunk; neither was I sober. A warm calm embraced me, as well as relief that the pain would soon be over. It was like standing at the end of a preposterously high diving board, looking down, and taking a couple of tentative bounces. Then you realize that climbing the ladder may have been the scariest part. The fourth cocktail went barely touched. I donned my coat and left a thirty dollar tip for the boyish bartender.

Stepping outside I beheld the most beautiful scene ever. The glistening snow was ankle-high and accumulating fast. Not a footprint anywhere. I trudged over to the main intersection of town where lights on the trees and storefronts resembled a snow globe. A flashing traffic light cast a pinkish hue. The snow-framed inn was magical. Standing in the middle of the road I turned my face to the sky, licking the fluffy dime-sized flakes.

The drive home was dicey, weaving left and right and sideways. I could make it only halfway up my sloped driveway. There were still some glowing embers in the hearth. I added a couple of logs.

I made a final tour of the house, all eleven rooms, imagining how the next owners would crassly undo all that Mireille and I had lovingly realized. Settling on the rug in front of the fireplace I poured a glass of bourbon. I do not really like bourbon. On a side table was my nasty knockout drug, Clozapine. My daily dose was one pill, 25 milligrams. If that dose could put me to sleep—and caused me to collapse on Fifth Avenue—a dozen should serenely finish the job. Without hesitation, I began popping a pill every three minutes. In what seemed to be more than half an hour, I passed out.

It was around noon when I opened my eyes and looked out. Everything was cottony and white. At first I thought I might be in heaven. There were bourbon stains on the rug and pills scattered about. My guess is I consumed up to 500mg. How could it be? Checking the drug online—something I should have done in advance—it turned out that some patients can take 500mg. I wasn't much of a reporter. I had always wondered how people could botch something as easy as suicide.

Several weeks later, on a painful Friday evening, and without fore-thought, I opted for a less reliable, though convenient, course of action.

With the garage door firmly shut, I arranged beach towels along the bottom to block any incoming air. As with the previous attempt, I was preternaturally calm, and disgusted. I started the engine and leaned back. Amost immediately, it turned very smoky and my eyes burned; I sat there three minutes . . . five minutes . . . ten minutes, then walked around the garage to examine the towels. I sat on the cement floor, eyes on fire. Time for an old fashioned. I probably should have researched that procedure, too.

CHAPTER 27
Lyme Disease

FOLLOWING MY BOTCHED ENDEAVORS IN Rhinebeck, I decided to return to therapy and pharmaceuticals, if even for six months. Around that time, I was offered an assignment from *Smithsonian* magazine to soak up the vinous majesty of the Champagne region in France. It was risky. I had not ventured to Europe for eight years, fearing a reprise of the nightmare vacation in Venice. Nonetheless I accepted, hoping for the best. In the past, with Anne or Mireille along, work trips were mini holidays of dining in multi-starred restaurants, sightseeing, shopping, and dropping in on family. But that trip would be all labor if you call drinking Champagne all day labor.

I had planned to pass the first two days in Paris, where, by chance, a friend was an executive at one of the world's most luxurious hotels, *Le Hôtel de Crillon*. He installed me in a breathtaking multi-room suite that could have accommodated a French rugby team. Tall windows framed the sculptural splendor of the city, while the waning autumn sun bathed my sitting room like a Vermeer landscape. I was delighted to be in Paris where, on my first visit in 1981, with Anne, I vowed that we would live there someday. Who knows, I ventured at the time, maybe I could be assigned to the *Times*' Paris bureau. For the next two days I planned to make the most of it: dining, museums, sampling wine bars, even though doing so alone would be poignant.

I hardly had time to shower and shave, for every five minutes someone knocked on the door to graciously bestow a gift: wine, mineral
water, a cheese plate, a fruit bowl, a guidebook, a tin of *foie gras*, a jar
of caviar. I dressed quickly, before they had a chance to usher in a
singing group.

Before leaving the room I sensed my metabolism revving up. It was
probably the jet lag. That was followed by shortness of breath, dizziness,
and cold hands, really cold hands. My feelings resembled a panic attack
but it wasn't a panic attack, I could tell. It was paired with fear, actually
terror, of something, maybe in the hotel room. I was very dizzy.

Within five minutes I was prone on the antique rug trying to catch
my breath. For the first time in my endless ordeal I believed I could
die, and be discovered by a staff member delivering another fruit bas-
ket. Strange, dark thoughts arose. In Rhinebeck I had always declared
that "they will carry me out" of my beloved farmhouse. I did not want
to be carried out of *Le Hôtel de Crillon*. I staggered across the room
and called Lucian, which probably added three hundred dollars to my
hotel bill. It was dinnertime in Newton, and he picked up right away.
He sounded alarmed and said he would try to fill a prescription for
Ambien or another tranquilizer at a Parisian pharmacy. That unfortunately proved too complicated. He told me to check my pulse.

"I don't know how to check my pulse!"

"Go to the nearest emergency room," Lucian commanded.

I flagged a hotel staff member and asked him to write down the
name of a nearby hospital and find me a cab.

In short order I was in an emergency room being administered oxy-
gen and injected with something I presume was a tranquilizer. A tall
young doctor with long black hair and a three-day beard held a stethoscope to my neck and heart. I explained my symptoms in elliptical
French. He called over a female colleague for another go-round with
the stethoscope. She asked what I had eaten in the past twenty-four
hours, and where I was staying. My choice of lodging made an impression, for she raised her eyebrows and later mentioned it to a nearby

assistant. I was remanded to a dim private room as the symptoms slowly subsided. The diagnosis was indeed a panic attack.

My guess was that the episode had something to do with being alone and far from home. I booked a return flight for the morning. Not to waste my only night in Paris, I walked along the *Rue de Rivoli*, stopping at one wine bar after another, until I reached *Le Halles* and one of my favorite restaurants. *Au Pied du Cochon* draws a fair share of tourists but is still an exhilarating, convivial, and consistently satisfying restaurant: red leather banquettes, floral wall panels, brash lighting, and nimble, swift, and good natured waiters. I always order the same specialties—oysters, grilled langoustines, and the house specialty, gelatinous, golden-fried pigs feet (And if you are still hungry, there is pig snout, chopped and fried).

Smithsonian was not pleased to have the story fall through; I told them I fell ill in Paris but that was it. Seven months later, I was asked by *Travel and Leisure* magazine to write an article on Lyon, the gastronomic capital of France—charcuterie, coq au vin, beef *Bourguignonne*, escargot, regional cheeses, and some of the best wines in the world. I hesitated to take the assignment, but decided I had to stare down the bear. Besides, my cycles had extended to nearly three weeks at a time. If I travelled strategically, it might be all right.

The trip went without incident. I spent much idyllic time in vineyards tasting the wines of *Beaujolais*, the *Mâconnais*, the *Côte Chalonnaise*, and others in northern Burgundy. While it would have been more enjoyable with companionship, I was simply grateful that a hospital was not on the itinerary.

My return home was what I refer to as the "There is a God" story.

My flight landed at Newark International Airport, two hours from Rhinebeck. The drive home took me close to Newton. I could stop and spend the night with my parents, or head home. As much as I wanted to drive home, something told me to overnight in Newton. They would like that, and I had not seen them in a while. It was one of the most momentous decisions of my life.

After dinner we settled in the den to watch a movie. When the film concluded, Lucian peered across the dark room and asked if I felt all right. I replied that I was very tired from the trip, which was understandable. Being a superb diagnostician, he read my body language and suspected there was something more. He fetched his stethoscope and placed it over my heart. A normal heart rate is between seventy and ninety beats per minute. Mine was seventeen. Startled, he located another stethoscope. When it confirmed my condition we hustled down to his private office in town where he administered an EKG test. It reported sixteen beats and losing altitude fast. I was dying.

At the hospital, everyone in the emergency room knew Lucian, so I drew a large, inquisitive gallery. They had not seen something quite like this. It was highly unlikely that a healthy forty-eight-year-old man would suffer a heart attack, and tests ruled that out. Infection? Inflammation? Medication? As my heart continued to wane one of the doctors hooked me up to an external pacemaker, which takes over for the ailing heart. The doctors whispered among themselves. I remember thinking that it might be best if they let nature take its course. I'd had enough. No one has so many brushes with death and walks away.

The youngest physician called out.

"Why not check him for Lyme disease?"

Blood was drawn and rushed to the lab.

Soon the technician returned.

"He's lit up like a Christmas tree with Lyme disease," he exclaimed. "Head to foot!"

The Lyme infection had caused something called heart block, in which an infection impedes electrical signals between the two chambers of the heart. There are three degrees of heart block:

1.   Very mild slowdown of the heart, not always noticeable
2.   Noticeable symptoms but still minor
3.   Extreme symptoms, sometimes fatal

Not unexpectedly, I was level three. There was never an E-ZPass in my lane.

The standard treatment for Lyme disease is antibiotics. If it is discovered in the first week or two it can be treated with a moderate dose. My infection likely had festered for six months or more. Because I lived alone and unwisely—stupidly—worked on the property wearing a T-shirt, I could have missed the telltale dartboard rash, particularly if it were on my back. The mid-Hudson Valley happens to be the Times Square of Lyme disease, which is carried by deer and rodent ticks.

In the hospital I was administered massive doses of antibiotics via a stent in the arm. As that was progressing, for good measure, I developed pneumonia. When it worsened the doctors came up with an entertaining treatment. As I sat up in the bed they threaded a tube through a hole in my back and into a lung, at which point they sucked out the noxious liquid. Twice.

After three days I was released with the stent remaining in my arm and returned to Rhinebeck. Many people with severe cases of Lyme disease suffer long-term issues like arthritic symptoms, extreme fatigue, dizziness, cognitive decline, vision impairment, and more. Remarkably, I made a complete recovery.

I asked Lucian what would have happened if I had not stopped to spend the night in Newton.

"You would have passed out at the wheel and crashed somewhere."

Lucian suggested that spending a month at the condo in West Palm Beach might perk me up. It was an invigorating change, swimming, dining out every evening. One morning while jogging along the Intracoastal Waterway, I detected a hissing in one of my ears—it appeared to be coming from my decorative ear. Tinnitus, again!

That evening, walking on the beach, I paused and gazed into the sky, shouting, "OK, don't stop now! Give me your best shot! Come on . . . hit me again, I'M STILL STANDING!!"

The following morning I drove five miles west to Riviera Beach, which has a tacky strip of mini malls, fast food outlets, bars, and pawn shops. Pawn shops sell guns. Simple, quick, foolproof. Why hadn't I thought of that method before? I entered one pawn shop and strutted up to a display case as if it were a regular outing for me.

There were snub-nosed gangster guns, squared off military guns, silver guns, *Lone Ranger* six-shooters, rifles, everything.

"What can I do for you?" asked the squat, drawling salesman.

"A gun."

"What kind?"

"Show me what you've got."

He produced a dozen models; they meant nothing to me.

"How about that one?"

He handed it over and I pretended to inspect it.

"I'll take it. Some bullets, too."

I felt some relief. I could not screw this up.

"License?" the salesman asked.

"Driver's license?"

"Gun license. From the state of your permanent residence."

"Oh shit."

CHAPTER 28
Soothsaying

NEW YORKERS LIVE INTENTLY IN the present with one cold eye fixed on the future. Tomorrow is where you want to be—in your career, your love life, and your circle of friends. I cared only about my future health. I had never set much store in fortune tellers; however a friend I trusted assured me Madame Bibi was the real deal.

In the 1980s, New York City was the soothsaying capital of America. Fortune tellers were plentiful in certain quarters of the city like the West Side (north of Times Square), the Upper East Side, the West Village, and the East Village. Not so much today, judging by the diminished presence of storefront practitioners. Then again, if you Google "psychic" you will discover a discreet and thriving astral trade: psychic tarot card readers, palmists, astrologers, spiritualists, telepathists, mediums, and others who subsist on the ever surging Niagara of urban angst.

My encounter with the occult came by chance. By that time my affliction had taken an unexpected turn: roughly three weeks of tap dancing exhilaration followed by two weeks in the brig. The medications continued to leave me trembling like a Parkinson's patient (or an alcoholic with the DT). I had always been a fast and accurate newspaper typist, but I now plodded along with one finger on the keyboard steadied by my left hand.

One evening I stopped by SoHo Kitchen and Bar, on Greene Street, to have a drink with a group of young thespians who had just put on a play in a nearby theater. One of them had been my clerk at the *Times*. Conversation centered around the flourishing downtown theater scene, about which I was ignorant since I'd hardly visited Manhattan for months aside from several work trips. One of the women began talking about a renowned fortune teller in Queens who was so extraordinary that clients came from three states, waiting as long as two months for a session.

I expressed great curiosity and asked her if I might sign up. Maybe a fortune teller could see things a psychotherapist could not.

"Better yet," she said. "I have an appointment for next Friday but I have to cancel. Why don't you go? Her name is Bibi."

"Oh, no," I said. 'You may change your mind."

"I insist."

Madame Bibi practiced her craft in an eyesore precinct of Queens, not a poor or rundown area, just architecturally offensive. The two-story brick home sat back from the street behind curlicues of white wrought iron. Shielding the walkway was another Queens residential motif—an aluminum canopy stretching from driveway to front door.

I was greeted by an attractive young woman in her twenties. That couldn't be Bibi. She led me through a cluttered living room where a TV blared and two little girls shrieked and laughed. By contrast, Bibi's lair was dim and serene. It was partitioned into a front room with a large window and round table, and in the back a small kitchen.

Bibi rose halfway to greet me. She was younger than expected, mid-fifties. Of average height and weight, she had a full round face, welcoming blue eyes, and reddish hair, most of which was concealed under a dark blue bandana. Her loose-fitting black sweater was offset by a long red sequined scarf and small gold amulet dangling from a neck chain. Her fingers were exceptionally long and smooth. She asked my name.

"Well, Bryan, what brought you here?"

I did not want to tell her that a girl I met in a bar gave me her ticket.

"I have heard many great things about you," I said.

"Well, we'll see. What are you interested in then, what aspect of your life would you like to explore? First, place your left palm on the table over the card."

Bibi's fields of scholarship were the past and the future, although if you were open to it, she could sprinkle in some general life advice.

"Family could be number one. Health two."

She split the deck and began rummaging through my attic of anxieties going back twenty years. Her observations on family were 75 percent on the mark. I had a sister who lived not too far away. I had no children. My mother had endured a marriage with a "difficult" man I did not care for.

She will be happy in her new life, she said. She would be fine.

"You are afraid of something."

I nodded sadly.

"It has been this way for a long time and causes great stress and problems with personal and professional relationships."

"Yes, yes."

The sole reason I had come to see Bibi, as I said, was to ascertain if my depression would go away. That is all I thought about twenty-four-hours a day. But suddenly I was not so sure I wanted to know many details, in the sense that I did not want to be told I would take the disease to the grave.

"This long-term illness is more of the spirit than the flesh. Your professional life has been very hard," she added, "but that will improve in the coming year."

"Can I look forward to total recovery?" I asked.

"Yes, that is for sure," she said. "You are already much healed but do not realize it. Try to be patient although I know it can be painful. Be kind to yourself."

Yes.

"Now you need to focus on neglected relationships. You are divorced?"

Yes.

"But you have a good relationship with her."

"Uh-huh."

I did not mention two divorces.

Bibi added that there were two women and maybe one man who were close to me but I had drifted from them. I should reconnect soon. They miss me.

"At this time I do not see immediate romantic interests. Stay close to your family."

She admonished me not to travel in the short term because it will only result in anxiety about leaving unfinished business at home.

"Why are your hands shaking?" she asked.

I explained.

The session lasted forty minutes and touched on nearly a dozen topics, both present and future. Bibi's performance was impressive, and I happily turned over thirty dollars. Regarding my illness, Bibi furnished enough level-headed observations and sound encouragement for one day. I would go back.

Chapter 29
Miracle on 181st Street

BY 2003 I WAS MAKING measured improvement, feeling well as much as 70 percent of the time, and with attenuated cycling. Years of therapy with Dr. Raskin had neutralized the stalking triggers. It was clear that every aspect of the depression was linked to the little kid and the trauma surrounding his father's disappearance, as well as his mother's reaction to it. Be that as it may, it was an anxious time.

The *Times* might have taken me back if it were not for the economic crisis facing all newspapers, which were hemorrhaging advertising revenue to internet enterprises like Craig's List. A few years earlier I had co-written a modestly profitable book called *Cooking for Dummies*, but it was not enough to support an extravagant city nightlife.

On one of my infrequent visits to Manhattan, I made the acquaintance of a tall, blonde-haired young woman named Amy, a magazine editor originally from Chicago. We began dining out in the city, usually on some publication's expense account. She came up to Rhinebeck and accompanied me on some out-of-town stories for the *New York Times*. It was nice to have company, even though we had virtually nothing in common apart from being journalists.

In the ensuing months finances deteriorated, and I was compelled to think the unthinkable: sell the Rhinebeck farmhouse. It would be like hocking my soul. On many evenings I would walk to the field behind the house and look back, saying to myself, *I own this big, wonderful place. I just have to get better.*

Three months later I found myself in a lawyer's office sitting across from a citified couple revealing their plans to purchase and remodel my house. They would probably take a paint roller to the magnificent hand-painted murals in the dining room, convert the cozy little library into a bedroom, and mess with my kitchen. Why did they tell me this? The husband had undergone a terribly disfiguring surgery that left a section of his jaw missing. He could hardly speak and had a sickly complexion. On second thought, I hoped that they *would* remodel, and that the unfortunate man would find some measure of peace, as I did, rocking on the front porch and watching the wild turkeys trot by.

Later that year, Amy and I moved to a railroad apartment in the Boerum Hill section of Brooklyn. I do not remember who brought up the notion of matrimony, although given my conjugal scorecard, I can't imagine it was me. I needed another wife like I needed cholera. But depression presents limited options: either you whine your way into submission, or you take it like a man. Moreover, when you are down, you are afraid to make decisions and afraid *not* to make decisions. Sometimes you just get into the canoe and let the other person paddle.

To be sure, fulfilling the "sickness and health" vow with a depressed spouse can be a trying affair, and some individuals are not morally or temperamentally capable of it. Anne and Mireille persevered for a long time and at great personal cost. I proffered my gratitude in my time tested way—by leaving them.

I had put off parenthood for twenty years because of the depression. Now in my early fifties, I had a younger partner who was hell-bent on having a child. After initial resistance, and to keep the peace, I half-heartedly went along with it. On April 13, 2005, we found ourselves driving to the maternity ward of New York-Presbyterian Hospital, three blocks from our apartment in Washington Heights. That morning I awoke feeling befogged and anxious; my mood was flatter than a poor man's wallet. Of all days. I wanted to kick a hole in the wall; but unlike the Peabody Hotel, ours were cinder blocks. We were led into a large, cheerful, pediatric wing of the hospital. The nurses and midwives were upbeat and amiable. Soon after my mother and Lucian arrived, Amy assumed her position on the raised bed. The midwife informed us that the world's population would not increase by one for about an hour, so we strolled around the neighborhood and stopped at a diner for coffee.

I told my parents that we had settled on a name. One evening while Amy and I were watching television I set some criteria: (1) Irish name. (2) Simple, not silly. (3) One syllable, convenient for shouting. Perfect: "Sean!"

We returned to the hospital just before kickoff. I remained detached and just wanted to leave. A midwife called me to take part in the procedure by holding one of Amy's legs. I demurred, but she insisted. It was not an easy waterslide getting Sean out, as he adopted the head first technique. It seemed like a week before he arrived.

What I am about to say will sound so improbable that readers will suspect I have fabricated it to create a dramatic ending to the book. Indeed, I hardly believe it myself. Sean was handed to me. Even in my much diminished state I was in awe of the slimy, squirming, little miracle. As I awkwardly cradled him in my arms, something astonishing occurred—my mind began to clear. That in itself was not remarkable; it had cleared, temporarily, hundreds of times when I was cycling. But this was different. I could not say why, but it was unlike any recovery I had experienced. It was like standing on a mountaintop and seeing all the way to Iceland.

I handed Sean to my mother and Lucian. We lingered for half an hour before I departed to retrieve the car, feeling better by the minute. A block out of the garage, I pulled over, pressed my head onto the steering wheel, and sighed:

"It's over. My God. It's over for good!" I have not experienced a debilitating day of depression since.

The cherubic new kid in Manhattan had vanquished the angry old kid from the Bronx. One question remained: Would this Lazarus act have occurred without medication and therapy? I believe not. It was the combination that teed up the ball, and I urge all who find themselves in the abyss to do the same.

Sean is now a towering sixteen-year-old, happy, sensitive, and kind. Even so, I will never shake the fear that the black bear could one day lean against his door. One hopes that there will soon be a pharmaceutical silver bullet. There was no silver bullet for the marriage, although Sean continues to enjoy the benefits of two parents in the same neighborhood. Cannot complain.

During much of that time I served as the nanny, or house husband—hey, I owed that kid, big time. The marriage was short-lived, and I moved on with my new life.

CHAPTER 30
Heaven

I HAD ALWAYS WONDERED WHERE my father, Skippy, was buried. My uncle Myles, who was married to Skippy's sister, Elaine, was one of the few extant relatives who had attended the funeral.

"It was the saddest thing I had ever seen," he remarked at a Christmas party at least fifteen years ago.

He mentioned something about a cemetery in Westchester. I launched a search. There are many cemeteries in Westchester, more than two dozen. I had to narrow the field. Being an Irish family, most likely it was a Catholic cemetery. There were eleven. Every Saturday I visited one and inquired in the records office, without luck. After eight expeditions, I considered calling off the hunt. Instead I dropped in on Gate of Heaven, a scenic setting of sloping wooded hills in the town of Valhalla.

The office was staffed by a small man with large glasses and pens in his shirt pocket. Behind him were rows of large ledger books arranged by year.

"What's the name and year?"

"Miller, Albert, 1955."

"OK, I'll be right back."

It was easy to locate.

"Miller, Miller ... Albert J."

He turned the ledger for me to read. All of the entrys were neatly hand written, like an eighteenth century land deed.

"Could you tell me where to find the grave?"

He took out a map and circled the area. I walked up the hill and became totally lost. I returned to the office where I was furnished with more detail and the number that is etched on every headstone. Why didn't he give me that the first time? Lost again, I followed the numbers but some appeared random. In a moment, in the shade of a red maple tree, there it was. It was a shotgun blast to the chest.

"Albert J. Miller. Loving Father and Husband." Thoughts turned to "the saddest thing" Myles had ever seen. I imagined the setting on that cold December day. While our family was small, their circle of friends, I presume, was sizable. It must have been too raw and heartbreaking to have a wake or other social function. I am certain my mother did bring me.

In my pocket was a photo of Sean that was wrapped in layers of aluminum foil. I had forgotten to bring something to dig with. I took out a pen and began excavating along the front of the stone. I placed the package in the little ditch and covered it with soil, telling my father all about his wonderful grandson. I told him I would return, and I have.

CHAPTER 31
The Last Dance

WE REFERRED TO LUCIAN AS the iron man for his robust health and imperturbable nature. He did not visit a doctor until he was eighty, when he came down with kidney stones during our stay in Florida. You could say he was a one man bucket brigade, always ready to rush to the scene of a family emergency, medical or otherwise. Lucian was among the last of the old time country general practitioners (He was also a cardiologist and onetime president of the New Jersey Heart Association). He told me that for decades he treated farmers in all corners of Sussex County. Some of them paid with vegetables, cakes, and moonshine.

When he retired, about fifteen years ago, his staff put on a reception in his little medical office in Newton. I drove down from Rhinebeck to attend. While looking for a parking space, I noticed a long line of people, nearly two blocks long, apparently waiting for a store clearance sale of some sort. It was Lucian's patients, past and present, coming to scold him for leaving them in the lurch, and fondly wishing him well. The majority of the attendees were older, and many carried gifts and food. A rangy old fellow with a deeply furrowed face came in and placed an envelope on the counter, then slipped out the back. Half an hour later someone spilled white wine on it. I grabbed the envelope and removed the contents. It was a greeting card holding an envelope.

Inside was a twenty dollar bill. "Thanks, doc," it said, "Gas for your airplane."

It was particularly distressing to see Lucian slide in his last two years, spending much of the time molded into a big chaise lounge in the den, watching reruns of New York Giants football games. In early 2017, he underwent what was described as minor sinus surgery. It was anything but. After that procedure, the apples began falling from the tree.

My mother's precipitous descent into dementia, a year before, was also horrendous considering her lifelong over-the-top vibrancy. And she went so fast. At breakfast she liked to look out the big bay window and identify colorful birds pecking at the feeder. When she stopped doing that, we knew dark clouds were blowing in. Dorothy began repeating herself and had difficulty finding words and names; within six months she passed into the agitation and fleeing phase, which is common. One night she bolted out of the house and was found at a nearby apple orchard. On another occasion she ran out to the road and, in her nightgown, somehow convinced a stranger to drive her to Newton Memorial Hospital, where Lucian was being treated.

The family decided to move her to Bristol Glen, in Newton, an upscale rehabilitation center with a well-regarded Alzheimer's/dementia center. The dementia wing smelled like mashed potatoes. It was colorful and clean and artsy-craftsy, like the set of *Sesame Street*, and was run by a cheerful, saintly staff. On my first visit, I watched three well-dressed women sitting at a game board, appearing almost normal; in an adjoining area was a gnarled, childlike woman hugging a doll and wailing loudly. Others busied themselves with art projects or simply gazed out the window. There were approximately twenty female residents, and one forlorn man. Alzheimer's disease and dementia—we never had her tested; what was the point?—afflicts women far more frequently than men. At the age of sixty-five, women have a one in five chance of developing the disorder compared with one out of eleven for men. My mother was eighty three.

Dorothy had a comfortable room with a TV and a modern bath, but she mostly remained in bed unless she was padding aimlessly around the premises. A fulltime aide mostly hung around and watched her sleep. Gradually she stopped eating regular meals and was fed protein shakes. When I last visited she appeared more annoyed than pleased, and did not seem to fully recognize me at first. I barely recognized her—shrunken, wrinkled, sickly pink, her once shimmering silver hair matted like a dog's rug, and wearing the hollow expression of a prisoner approaching the electric chair.

How pitiful. Here is the person who spoon fed you, picked up your clothes, organized birthday parties, made soup when you were sick, attended ball games, beamed at graduation, and sobbed at your wedding. And now, at times you could be the janitor for all she knows. It's a shotgun blast to the chest.

Sitting in her ninety-nine-degree room, I thought of some crazy things that we used to laugh about: The Thanksgiving when she placed the cooked turkey in the garage to cool and our dog Josephine dragged it into the woods. Or the Christmas when, before the guests arrived, I got so drunk on her strong eggnog that I stretched out on my bed and awoke on December 26. For years, whenever I left the house to go to Rhinebeck, she called out that she and Lucian were so happy at my departure that they could "tap dance on the driveway." And they did.

Though he was increasingly weak, Lucian stubbornly insisted upon remaining in the house. He was tended to by an affable male caretaker from Saint Lucia who demonstrated his gratitude for employment by breaking into the upstairs safe and spiriting off with more than fifty thousand dollars' worth of jewelry. Eventually Lucian was admitted to Bristol Glen's "rehabilitation unit," though there was little left to rehabilitate. He was on the floor above his wife. Even in her opaque state, my mother harassed the staff into taking her to see him at least once a day. I have never seen a couple so in love. When she was with him, she was more aware, walked almost normally, and held his hand.

I could not help thinking that for once I was the healthy one in the room trying to comfort others.

In early 2017, there was a large event in Lucian's honor at the Karen Ann Quinlan Hospice Center, in Newton. Quinlan was the young woman at the focus of a national right-to-die legal dispute that went all the way to the Supreme Court. After ten years in a coma—1975 to 1985—and having been maintained on life support, her parents requested that doctors pull the plug. Lucian was on duty when she arrived at the hospital. Opponents of the move filed a legal action. In the end the family prevailed.

Lucian was a founder of the organization and remained involved until he fell ill. We took a risk and brought my mother to the event—she was all but silent, bewildered, with a searching, childlike expression. But she seemed to recognize me on some level, I could tell. I reflected on how, for all of my life, I never told her I loved her. And it troubled her. She called me out on it during our calamitous drive to Rhinebeck.

Dorothy was always a snappy dresser, and we made sure she was smartly attired and wearing some of her (remaining) nice jewelry. A number of Lucian's family members joined us at a large round table. Lucian was asked to say a few words. Hunched, frail, and rasping, he soldiered through for two minutes, to energetic applause. It would be his final doctor's call.

Following the meal, music resounded from across the room, and soon the dance floor was full. I hoped that my mother would find a tiny morsel of pleasure in watching the guests, many of whom she had known for decades. Suddenly, she reached over and took my hand, squeezing it gently. Rising from the table, she led me onto the dance floor as the family watched, flabbergasted. It was the old Dorothy, slower of course, and minus her trademark "Whew!" A lady dancing nearby with her husband looked over and flashed an air kiss. She was in tears. My mother clasped my hands and swung them from side to side in a hammock motion. Yes, she used to say I danced like Frankenstein, and this was on full display at the moment.

A slow song followed. I placed one hand over her skeletal frame and we circled slowly, her leading and me, lumbering to keep up. This was the last dance. I should have been overwhelmed with emotions, but strangely was not, and believe me, I tried. Of course I loved my mother, but I could not say it to her, not even as the final notes of the final song of our final dance wafted over the room. The kid from the Bronx, though essentially defeated, would not allow it.

I steadied Dorothy by the shoulders. She stepped back, looked down at my shoes, then uttered the last word I would ever hear from her.

"Bad."

Epilogue

IT IS SAID THAT ONLY those who have suffered grave illness, and recovered, can experience true happiness. As I sit here in a closet-size home office, fifteen years out from my Iditarod of despair, I concede that this proposition carries a modicum of truth. I revel in well-being, even on a no-frills basis. But it took some time.

Depression is not a room you walk out of. When confined inside, you are never aware of when or if you will be let free, and that takes a tremendous toll—a kidnapping without a ransom note. For those emerging from the affliction, happiness runs on its own timetable.

So am I experiencing true happiness? Maybe, in a backwards sort of way. I have been waterboarded so many times that virtually nothing, aside from harm to my sixteen-year-old son Sean, can rattle me. And I have lots to rattle about.

The "black bear," as I called the malady, made off with my wallet, my career, my home, my savings, and a good number of friends and acquaintances. A beautiful seven-bedroom farmhouse on five lush acres vanished like a sand castle on a rising tide. Today I dwell in a small apartment that is roughly the size of my first domicile following college—and *that* was small. Finances have allowed but one vacation in more than a decade, when I took then ten-year-old Sean to Club Med, in the Caribbean. It was heaven.

My emotional parole coincided with a steady decline in the

American newspaper industry, thanks to the internet. Moreover, I was approaching an age—and salary level—that pushed me close to the superannuated bin. In New York City, of all places, you do not want to fall off the carousel. It will just keep going. So with depression, you cut the best deal you can, and move on. No sense whining. I continue to take Dr. Liebowitz's cocktail to address lingering biochemical deficiencies; there is no longer a need for therapy. If today is as good as it gets, well, punch my ticket and point me toward the fun house.

If there is a singular takeaway from this book, it is this: Childhood experiences, at no matter what age, are infinitely more powerful and enduring than one can imagine. Indelible tattoos. Following the death of my father, I hauled around a time bomb on a thirty-year trigger. How could this be? Thirty years? Upon entering psychotherapy for the first time, I kicked back at this notion. To the doctor I protested that I was three-years-old when the tragedy occurred. I recalled nothing. I recalled everything. When Sean reached age three, I observed him playing in the living room and laughing at me, and wondered what would happen if I were to pack a bag and move to Portugal, permanently. The answer was pretty clear.

Recuperation is both spiritual and physical. Depression, like other life-threatening infirmities, brings out the prayer book in all of us. We plead and beg and promise that, if health is restored, the deity will be reimbursed with five visits a day (name your religion) to a house of worship. Don't count on it.

I was not keen on writing this book. My battalion of faults has ample troopers; no need to dig up more. One day I was in my agent's office, unsure of whether this project would be of interest to anyone aside from depressed people. It was decided yes, providing that I pull open the sluice gates and let it flow.

To a substantial degree, this book is about women in my life—lots of them. I don't know what to say. They were admirable people who just happened to wander into the wrong neighborhood. If I deserve to face charges, it is for the malefactions in my first two marriages. Anne and

Mireille selflessly held my hand through the worst of the plague, while putting their own lives and careers on hold. They were rewarded with heartbreak and abandonment, something I atone for, literally, every day. If there is any consolation, it is that they understand the dark circumstances in which it occurred and have forgiven me. They remain in my world—Anne in France and Mireille in New York City. I am frequently in touch with both of them; three years ago I spent part of a summer vacation with Anne at the family estate, Soustres.

I miss the *New York Times*, terribly. It never crossed my mind that I would ever leave. At my job interview with the executive editor, Abe Rosenthal, he made a point of calculating my renumeration if I remained on staff for thirty years.

"You are aware that when someone comes to the *Times* they never leave the *Times*."

He didn't have to tell me that. I was so thrilled to be there I would have happily vacuumed the newsroom every night after deadline.

And during my time there it felt like family; I do not know why, but it did. Of course I was a privileged character, the professional eater, pockets bulging with currency. It was not uncommon for me to write three-to-four-thousand words a week—when I was not suicidally ill. I continue to write for the paper as a freelancer, but it is not the same. Some of the editors, many half my age, do not know and don't care who I am. Why would they?

Still, what a relief being able to read and laugh and converse and enter meeting rooms that are not filled with vampires.

Another relief: I no longer have to lie. Like riverboat gamblers, depressives lie all day: about their moods, nasty medications, disappearing acts, social excuses. And we are damned good at it.

Having survived depression, I feel an obligation to give back. I am no therapist, however I can relate to the afflicted in ways no professional can. Dr. Raskin, my psychotherapist, is brilliant, but I always wished that he—and his professional colleagues—could live one day with serious depression; actually, one hour would do the trick. They would never be the same. Three years ago I organized a revolving help group of eight to nine people, and all have found it tremendously positive. No lying required.

Something unexpected and revealing has transpired in the past two months. The publisher of this book issued an online publicity notice, presumably to book sellers and the media. It summarizes the story, warts and all, and divulges how the illness destroyed my personal and professional lives. Eagerly, I forwarded the release to about thirty friends and acquaintances. About one third of them responded with congratulations; another third did not respond for weeks, and when they did hardly mentioned the book; the remaining third grabbed their hats and ran for the hills. Not a single one has answered, and that includes some relatives.

As I note in the book, for more than ten years, as a renowned (and virtually the only) restaurant critic in New York, I was a flickering candle that lured scores of social moths. Now I am a moth. Yet I am reacquainted with life. The universe is a good place.